Lecture Notes in Computer Science 4499

Commenced Publication in 1973
Founding and Former Series Editors:
Gerhard Goos, Juris Hartmanis, and Jan van Leeuwen

Yun Q. Shi (Ed.)

Transactions on Data Hiding and Multimedia Security II

 Springer

Volume Editor

Yun Q. Shi
New Jersey Institute of Technology
Department of Electrical and Computer Engineering
323, M.L. King Blvd., Newark, NJ 07102, USA
E-mail: shi@njit.edu

Library of Congress Control Number: 2007928444

CR Subject Classification (1998): K.4.1, K.6.5, H.5.1, D.4.6, E.3, E.4, F.2.2, H.3, I.4

LNCS Sublibrary: SL 4 – Security and Cryptology

ISSN   0302-9743 (Lecture Notes in Computer Science)
ISSN   1864-3043 (Transactions on Data Hiding and Multimedia Security)
ISBN-10   3-540-73091-5 Springer Berlin Heidelberg New York
ISBN-13   978-3-540-73091-0 Springer Berlin Heidelberg New York

Springer is a part of Springer Science+Business Media

springer.com

© Springer-Verlag Berlin Heidelberg 2007
Printed in Germany

Typesetting: Camera-ready by author, data conversion by Scientific Publishing Services, Chennai, India
Printed on acid-free paper   SPIN: 12077731   06/3180   5 4 3 2 1 0

Preface

In this volume we present the second issue of the *LNCS Transactions on Data Hiding and Multimedia Security*.

In the first paper, Adelsbach et al. introduce fingercasting, a combination of broadcast encryption and fingerprinting for secure content distribution. They also provide for the first time a security proof for a lookup table-based encryption scheme. In the second paper, He and Kirovski propose an estimation attack on content-based video fingerprinting schemes. Although the authors tailor the attack towards a specific video fingerprint, the generic form of the attack is expected to be applicable to a wide range of video watermarking schemes. In the third paper, Ye et al. present a new feature distance measure for error-resilient image authentication, which allows one to differentiate maliciousimage manipulations from changes that do not interfere with the semantics of an image. In the fourth paper, Luo et al. present a steganalytic technique against steganographic embedding methods utilizing the two least significant bit planes. Experimental results demonstrate that this steganalysis method can reliably detect embedded messages and estimate their length with high precision. Finally, Alface and Macq present a comprehensive survey on blind and robust 3-D shape watermarking.

We hope that this issue is of great interest to the research community and will trigger new research in the field of data hiding and multimedia security.

Finally, we want to thank all the authors, reviewers and editors who devoted their valuable time to the success of this second issue. Special thanks go to Springer and Alfred Hofmann for their continuous support.

March 2007

Yun Q. Shi
(Editor-in-Chief)
Hyoung-Joong Kim
(Vice Editor-in-Chief)
Stefan Katzenbeisser
(Vice Editor-in-Chief)

Table of Contents

Fingercasting–Joint Fingerprinting and Decryption of Broadcast
Messages.. 1
    André Adelsbach, Ulrich Huber, and Ahmad-Reza Sadeghi

An Estimation Attack on Content-Based Video Fingerprinting......... 35
    Shan He and Darko Kirovski

Statistics- and Spatiality-Based Feature Distance Measure for Error
Resilient Image Authentication 48
    Shuiming Ye, Qibin Sun, and Ee-Chien Chang

LTSB Steganalysis Based on Quartic Equation...................... 68
    Xiangyang Luo, Chunfang Yang, Daoshun Wang, and Fenlin Liu

From 3D Mesh Data Hiding to 3D Shape Blind and Robust
Watermarking: A Survey... 91
    Patrice Rondao Alface and Benoit Macq

Author Index.. 117

Fingercasting–Joint Fingerprinting and Decryption of Broadcast Messages*

André Adelsbach, Ulrich Huber, and Ahmad-Reza Sadeghi

Horst Görtz Institute for IT Security
Ruhr-Universität Bochum
Universitätsstraße 150
D-44780 Bochum
Germany
andre.adelsbach@nds.rub.de, {huber,sadeghi}@crypto.rub.de

Abstract. We propose a stream cipher that provides confidentiality, traceability and renewability in the context of broadcast encryption assuming that collusion-resistant watermarks exist. We prove it to be as secure as the generic pseudo-random sequence on which it operates. This encryption approach, termed fingercasting, achieves joint decryption and fingerprinting of broadcast messages in such a way that an adversary cannot separate both operations or prevent them from happening simultaneously. The scheme is a combination of a known broadcast encryption scheme, a well-known class of fingerprinting schemes and an encryption scheme inspired by the Chameleon cipher. It is the first to provide a formal security proof and a non-constant lower bound for resistance against collusion of malicious users, i.e., a minimum number of content copies needed to remove all fingerprints. To achieve traceability, the scheme fingerprints the receivers' key tables such that they embed a fingerprint into the content during decryption. The scheme is efficient and includes parameters that allow, for example, to trade-off storage size for computation cost at the receiving end.

Keywords: Chameleon encryption, stream cipher, spread-spectrum watermarking, fingerprinting, collusion resistance, frame-proofness, broadcast encryption.

1 Introduction

Experience shows that adversaries attack Broadcast Encryption (BE) systems in a variety of different ways. Their attacks may be on the hardware that stores cryptographic keys, e.g., when they extract keys from a compliant device to develop a pirate device such as the DeCSS software that circumvents the Content Scrambling System [2]. Alternatively, their attacks may be on the decrypted content, e.g., when a legitimate user shares decrypted content with illegitimate users on a file sharing system such as Napster, Kazaa, and BitTorrent.

---

* An extended abstract of this paper appeared in the Proceedings of the Tenth Australasian Conference on Information Security and Privacy (ACISP 2006) [1].

Y.Q. Shi (Eds.): Transactions on DHMS II, LNCS 4499, pp. 1–34, 2007.

The broadcasting sender thus has three security requirements: *confidentiality*, *traceability* of content and keys, and *renewability* of the encryption scheme. The requirements cover two aspects. Confidentiality tries to prevent illegal copies in the first place, whereas traceability is a second line of defense aimed at finding the origin of an illegal copy (content or key). The need for traceability originates from the fact that confidentiality may be compromised in rare cases, e.g., when a few users illegally distribute their secret keys. Renewability ensures that after such rare events, the encryption system can recover from the security breach.

In broadcasting systems deployed today, e.g., Content Protection for Pre-Recorded Media [3] or the Advanced Access Content System [4], confidentiality and renewability often rely on BE because it provides short ciphertexts while at the same time having realistic storage requirements in devices and acceptable computational overhead. Traitor tracing enables traceability of keys, whereas fingerprinting provides traceability of content. Finally, renewability may be achieved using revocation of the leaked keys.

However, none of the mentioned cryptographic schemes covers all three security requirements. Some existing BE schemes lack traceability of keys, whereas no practically relevant scheme provides traceability of content [5,6,7,8]. Traitor tracing only provides traceability of keys, but not of content [9,10]. Fingerprinting schemes alone do not provide confidentiality [11]. The original Chameleon cipher provides confidentiality, traceability and a hint on renewability, but with a small constant bound for collusion resistance and, most importantly, without formal proof of security [12]. Asymmetric schemes, which provide each compliant device with a certificate and accompany content with Certificate Revocation Lists (CRLs), lack traceability of content and may reach the limits of renewability when CRLs become too large to be processed by real-world devices. Finally, a trivial combination of fingerprinting and encryption leads to an unacceptable transmission overhead because the broadcasting sender needs to sequentially transmit each fingerprinted copy.

Our Contribution. We present, to the best of our knowledge, the first rigorous security proof of Chameleon ciphers, thus providing a sound foundation for the recent applications of these ciphers, e.g., [13]. Furthermore, we give an explicit criterion to judge the security of the Chameleon cipher's key table. Our *fingercasting* approach fulfills all three security requirements at the same time. It is a combination of (i) a new Chameleon cipher based on the *finger*printing capabilities of a well-known class of watermarking schemes and (ii) an arbitrary broad*cast* encryption scheme, which explains the name of the approach. The basic idea is to use the Chameleon cipher for combining decryption and fingerprinting. To achieve renewability, we use a BE scheme to provide fresh session keys as input to the Chameleon scheme. To achieve traceability, we fingerprint the receivers' key tables such that they embed a fingerprint into the content during decryption. To enable higher collusion resistance than the original Chameleon scheme, we tailor our scheme to emulate any watermarking scheme whose coefficients follow a probability distribution that can be disaggregated into additive components.[1] As proof of concept, we instantiate the watermarking scheme with Spread Spectrum Watermarking (SSW), which has proven collusion resistance [14,15]. However, we might as well instantiate it with any other such scheme.

Joint decryption and fingerprinting has significant advantages compared to existing methods such as transmitter-side or receiver-side Fingerprint Embedding (FE) [11]. Transmitter-side FE is the trivial combination of fingerprinting and encryption by the sender. As discussed above, the transmission overhead is in the order of the number of copies to be distributed, which is prohibitive in practical applications. Receiver-side FE happens in the user's receiver; after distribution of a single encrypted copy of the content, a secure receiver based on tamper-resistant hardware is trusted to embed the fingerprint *after* decryption. This saves bandwidth on the broadcast channel. However, perfect tamper-resistance cannot be achieved under realistic assumptions [16]. An adversary may succeed in extracting the keys of a receiver and subsequently decrypt without embedding a fingerprint.

Our fingercasting approach combines the advantages of both methods. It saves bandwidth by broadcasting a single encrypted copy of the content. In addition, it ensures embedding of a fingerprint even if a malicious user succeeds in extracting the decryption keys of a receiver. Furthermore, as long as the number of colluding users remains below a threshold, the colluders can only create decryption keys and content copies that incriminate at least one of them.

This paper enhances our extended abstract [1] in the following aspects. First, the extended abstract does not contain the security proof, which is the major contribution. Second, we show here that our instantiation of SSW is exact, whereas the extended abstract only claims this result. Last, we discuss here the trade-off between storage size and computation cost at the receiving end.

2   Related Work

The original Chameleon cipher of Anderson and Manifavas is 3-collusion-resistant [12]: A collusion of up to 3 malicious users has a negligible chance of creating a good copy that does not incriminate them. Each legitimate user knows the seed of a Pseudo-Random Sequence (PRS) and a long table filled with random keywords. Based on the sender's master table, each receiver obtains a slightly different table copy, where individual bits in the keywords are modified in a characteristic way. Interpreting the PRS as a sequence of addresses in the table, the sender adds the corresponding keywords in the master table bitwise modulo 2 in order to mask the plaintext word. The receiver applies the same operation to the ciphertext using its table copy, thus embedding the fingerprint.

The original cipher, however, has some inconveniences. Most importantly, it has no formal security analysis and bounds the collusion resistance by the constant number 3, whereas our scheme allows to choose this bound depending on the number of available watermark coefficients. In addition, the original scheme

---

[1] Our scheme does not yet support fingerprints based on coding theory.

limits the content space (and keywords) to strings with characteristic bit positions that may be modified without visibly altering the content. In contrast, our scheme uses algebraic operations in a group of large order, which enables modification of any bit in the keyword and processing of arbitrary documents.

Chameleon was inspired by work from Maurer [17,18]. His cipher achieves information-theoretical security in the bounded storage model with high probability. In contrast, Chameleon and our proposed scheme only achieve computational security. The reason is that the master table length in Maurer's cipher is super-polynomial. As any adversary would need to store most of the table to validate guesses, the bounded storage capacity defeats all attacks with high probability. However, Maurer's cipher was never intended to provide traceability of content or renewability, but only confidentiality.

Ferguson et al. discovered security weaknesses in a randomized stream cipher similar to Chameleon [19]. However, their attack only works for linear sequences of keywords in the master table, not for the PRSs of our proposed solution.

Ergun, Kilian, and Kumar prove that an averaging attack with additional Gaussian noise defeats any watermarking scheme [20]. Their bound on the minimum number of different content copies needed for the attack asymptotically coincides with the bound on the maximum number of different content copies to which the watermarking scheme of Kilian et al. is collusion-resistant [15]. As we can emulate [15] with our fingercasting approach, its collusion resistance is—at least asymptotically—the best we can hope for.

Recently there was a great deal of interest in joint fingerprinting and decryption [13,21,22,11,23]. Basically, we can distinguish three strands of work. The first strand of work applies Chameleon in different application settings. Briscoe et al. introduce Nark, which is an application of the original Chameleon scheme in the context of Internet multicast [13]. However, in contrast to our new Chameleon cipher they neither enhance Chameleon nor analyze its security. The second strand of work tries to achieve joint fingerprinting and decryption by either trusting network nodes to embed fingerprints (Watercasting in [21]) or doubling the size of the ciphertext by sending differently fingerprinted packets of content [22]. Our proposed solution neither relies on trusted network nodes nor increases the ciphertext size. The third strand of work proposes new joint fingerprinting and decryption processes, but at the price of replacing encryption with scrambling, which does not achieve indistinguishability of ciphertext and has security concerns [11,23]. In contrast, our new Chameleon cipher achieves indistinguishability of ciphertext.

3   Preliminaries

3.1   Notation

We recall some standard notations that will be used throughout the paper. First, we denote scalar objects with lower-case variables, e.g., o_1, and object tuples as well as roles with upper-case variables, e.g., X_1. When we summarize objects or roles in set notation, we use an upper-case calligraphic variable, e.g., $\mathcal{O} := \{o_1, o_2, \ldots\}$ or $\mathcal{X} := \{X_1, X_2, \ldots\}$. Second, let A be an algorithm. By $y \leftarrow \mathsf{A}(x)$ we denote that y was obtained by running A on input x. If A is deterministic, then y is a variable with a unique value. Conversely, if A is probabilistic, then y is a random variable. For example, by $y \leftarrow \mathsf{N}(\mu, \sigma)$ we denote that y was obtained by selecting it at random with normal distribution, where μ is the mean and σ the standard deviation. Third, $o_1 \xleftarrow{R} \mathcal{O}$ and $o_2 \xleftarrow{R} [0, z]$ denote the selection of a random element of the set $\mathcal{O}$ and the interval $[0, z]$ with uniform distribution. Finally, $V \cdot W$ denotes the dot product of two vectors $V := (v_1, \ldots, v_n)$ and $W := (w_1, \ldots, w_n)$, which is defined as $V \cdot W := \sum_{j=1}^{n} v_j w_j$, while $\|V\|$ denotes the Euclidean norm $\|V\| := \sqrt{V \cdot V}$.

3.2   Roles and Objects in Our System Model

The *(broadcast) center* manages the broadcast channel, distributes decryption keys and is fully trusted. The *users* obtain the content via devices that we refer to as *receivers*. For example, a receiver may be a set-top box in the context of pay-TV or a DVD player in movie distribution. We denote the number of receivers with N; the set of receivers is $\mathcal{U} := \{u_i \mid 1 \le i \le N\}$. When a receiver violates the terms and conditions of the application, e.g., leaks its keys or shares content, the center revokes the receiver's keys and thus makes them useless for decryption purposes. We denote the set of revoked receivers with $\mathcal{R} := \{r_1, r_2, \ldots\} \subset \mathcal{U}$.

We represent broadcast content as a sequence $M := (m_1, \ldots, m_n)$ of real numbers in $[0, z]$, where M is an element of the content space $\mathcal{M}$.[2] For example, these numbers may be the n most significant coefficients of the Discrete Cosine Transform (DCT) as described in [14]. However, they should not be thought of as a literal description of the underlying content, but as a representation of the values that are to be changed by the watermarking process [20]. We refer to these values as *significant* and to the remainder as *insignificant*. In the remainder of this paper, we only refer to the significant part of the content, but briefly comment on the insignificant part in Section 5.

3.3   Cryptographic Building Blocks

Negligible Function. A negligible function $\mathsf{f} : \mathbb{N} \to \mathbb{R}$ is a function where the inverse of any polynomial is asymptotically an upper bound:

$$\forall k > 0 \; \exists \lambda_0 \; \forall \lambda > \lambda_0 : \quad \mathsf{f}(\lambda) < 1/\lambda^k$$

Probabilistic Polynomial Time. A probabilistic polynomial-time algorithm is an algorithm for which there exists a polynomial poly such that for every input $x \in \{0, 1\}^*$ the algorithm always halts after $\mathsf{poly}(|x|)$ steps, independently of the outcome of its internal coin tosses.

---

[2] Although this representation mainly applies to images, we discuss an extension to movies and songs in Section 5.

Pseudo-Random Sequence (PRS). We first define the notion of pseudo-randomness and then proceed to define a Pseudo-Random Sequence Generator (PRSG). For further details we refer to [24, Section 3.3.1]:

Definition 1 (Pseudo-randomness). *Let* $\mathsf{len} : \mathbb{N} \to \mathbb{N}$ *be a polynomial such that* $\mathsf{len}(\lambda) > \lambda$ *for all* $\lambda \in \mathbb{N}$ *and let* $U_{\mathsf{len}(\lambda)}$ *be a random variable uniformly distributed over the strings* $\{0, 1\}^{\mathsf{len}(\lambda)}$ *of length* $\mathsf{len}(\lambda)$*. Then the random variable* X *with* $|X| = \mathsf{len}(\lambda)$ *is called* pseudo-random *if for every probabilistic polynomial-time distinguisher* $\mathcal{D}$*, the advantage* $\mathsf{Adv}\,(\lambda)$ *is a negligible function:*

$$\mathsf{Adv}\,(\lambda) := \left| \Pr\left[\mathcal{D}(X) = 1\right] - \Pr\left[\mathcal{D}(U_{\mathsf{len}(\lambda)}) = 1\right] \right|$$

Definition 2 (Pseudo-Random Sequence Generator). *A* PRSG *is a deterministic polynomial-time algorithm* G *that satisfies two requirements:*

1. *Expansion: There exists a polynomial* $\mathsf{len} : \mathbb{N} \to \mathbb{N}$ *such that* $\mathsf{len}(\lambda) > \lambda$ *for all* $\lambda \in \mathbb{N}$ *and* $|\mathsf{G}(str)| = \mathsf{len}(|str|)$ *for all* $str \in \{0, 1\}^*$*.*
2. *Pseudo-randomness: The random variable* $\mathsf{G}(U_\lambda)$ *is pseudo-random.*

A PRS *is a sequence* $\mathsf{G}(str)$ *derived from a uniformly distributed random seed* str *using a PRSG.*

Chameleon Encryption. To set up a Chameleon scheme $\mathcal{CE} := (\mathsf{KeyGenCE}, \mathsf{KeyExtrCE}, \mathsf{EncCE}, \mathsf{DecCE}, \mathsf{DetectCE})$, the center generates the secret master table MT, the secret table fingerprints $TF := (TF^{(1)}, \ldots, TF^{(N)})$, and selects a threshold t using the key generation algorithm $(MT, TF, t) \leftarrow \mathsf{KeyGenCE}(N, 1^{\lambda'}, par_{\mathsf{CE}})$, where N is the number of receivers, λ' a security parameter, and par_{CE} a set of performance parameters. To add receiver u_i to the system, the center uses the key extraction algorithm $RT^{(i)} \leftarrow \mathsf{KeyExtrCE}(MT, TF, i)$ to deliver the secret receiver table $RT^{(i)}$ to u_i. To encrypt content M exclusively for the receivers in possession of a receiver table $RT^{(i)}$ and a fresh session key k^{sess}, the center uses the encryption algorithm $C \leftarrow \mathsf{EncCE}(MT, k^{\mathsf{sess}}, M)$, where the output is the ciphertext C. Only a receiver u_i in possession of $RT^{(i)}$ and k^{sess} is capable of decrypting C and obtaining a fingerprinted copy $M^{(i)}$ of content M using the decryption algorithm $M^{(i)} \leftarrow \mathsf{DecCE}(RT^{(i)}, k^{\mathsf{sess}}, C)$.

When the center discovers an illegal copy M^* of content M, it executes $\mathsf{DetectCE}$, which uses the fingerprint detection algorithm $\mathsf{DetectFP}$ of the underlying fingerprinting scheme to detect whether $RT^{(i)}$ left traces in M^*. For further details on our notation of a Chameleon scheme, we refer to Appendix C.

Fingerprinting. To set up a fingerprinting scheme, the center generates the secret content fingerprints $CF := (CF^{(1)}, \ldots, CF^{(N)})$ and the secret similarity threshold t using the setup algorithm $(CF, t) \leftarrow \mathsf{SetupFP}(N, n', par_{\mathsf{FP}})$, where N is the number of receivers, n' the number of content coefficients, and par_{FP} a set of performance parameters. To embed the content fingerprint $CF^{(i)} := (cf_1^{(i)}, \ldots, cf_{n'}^{(i)})$ of receiver u_i into the original content M, the center uses the embedding algorithm $M^{(i)} \leftarrow \mathsf{EmbedFP}(M, CF^{(i)})$. To verify whether an illegal copy M^* of content M contains traces of the content fingerprint $CF^{(i)}$ of receiver

u_i, the center uses the detection algorithm $dec \leftarrow \mathsf{DetectFP}(M, M^*, CF^{(i)}, t)$. It calculates the similarity between the detected fingerprint $CF^* := M^* - M$ and $CF^{(i)}$ using a similarity measure. If the similarity is above the threshold t, then the center declares u_i guilty ($dec = \mathtt{true}$), otherwise innocent ($dec = \mathtt{false}$). This type of detection algorithm is called non-blind because it needs the original content M as input; the opposite is a blind detection algorithm.

We call a fingerprinting scheme *additive* if the probability distribution ProDis of its coefficients has the following property: Adding two independent random variables that follow ProDis results in a random variable that also follows ProDis. For example, the normal distribution has this property, where the means and variances add up during addition.

Spread Spectrum Watermarking (SSW) is an instance of an additive fingerprinting scheme. We describe the SSW scheme of [15], which we later use to achieve collusion resistance. The content fingerprint $CF^{(i)}$ consists of independent random variables $cf_j^{(i)}$ with normal distribution $\mathsf{ProDis} = \mathsf{N}(0, \sigma')$, where σ' is a function $\mathsf{f}_{\sigma'}(N, n', par_{\mathsf{FP}})$. The similarity threshold t is a function $\mathsf{f}_t(\sigma', N, par_{\mathsf{FP}})$. Both functions $\mathsf{f}_{\sigma'}$ and f_t are specified in [15]. During $\mathsf{EmbedFP}$, the center adds the fingerprint coefficients to the content coefficients: $m_j^{(i)} \leftarrow m_j + cf_j^{(i)}$. The similarity test is $\mathsf{Sim}(CF^*, CF^{(i)}) \geq t$ with $\mathsf{Sim}(CF^*, CF^{(i)}) := (CF^* \cdot CF^{(i)})/\|CF^*\|$. Finally, the scheme's security is given by:

Theorem 1. [15, Section 3.4] *In the SSW scheme with the above parameters, an adversarial coalition needs $\Omega(\sqrt{n'/\ln N})$ differently fingerprinted copies of content M to have a non-negligible chance of creating a good copy M^* without any coalition member's fingerprint.*

For further details on our notation of a fingerprinting scheme and the SSW scheme of [15], we refer to Appendix D.

Broadcast Encryption. To set up the scheme, the center generates the secret master key MK using the key generation algorithm $MK \leftarrow \mathsf{KeyGenBE}(N, 1^{\lambda''})$, where N is the number of receivers and λ'' the security parameter. To add receiver u_i to the system, the center uses the key extraction algorithm $SK^{(i)} \leftarrow \mathsf{KeyExtrBE}(MK, i)$ to extract the secret key $SK^{(i)}$ of u_i. To encrypt session key k^{sess} exclusively for the non-revoked receivers $\mathcal{U} \setminus \mathcal{R}$, the center uses the encryption algorithm $C \leftarrow \mathsf{EncBE}(MK, \mathcal{R}, k^{\mathsf{sess}})$, where the output is the ciphertext C. Only a non-revoked receiver u_i has a matching private key $SK^{(i)}$ that allows to decrypt C and obtain k^{sess} using the decryption algorithm $k^{\mathsf{sess}} \leftarrow \mathsf{DecBE}(i, SK^{(i)}, C)$. For further details on our notation of a BE scheme, we refer to Appendix E.

3.4 Requirements of a Fingercasting Scheme

Before we enter into the details of our fingercasting approach, we summarize its requirements: correctness, security, collusion resistance, and frame-proofness. To put it simply, the aim of our fingercasting approach is to generically combine an instance of a BE scheme, a Chameleon scheme, and a fingerprinting scheme such that the combination inherits the security of BE and Chameleon as well as the collusion resistance of fingerprinting. To define correctness we first need to clarify how intrusive a fingerprint may be. For a copy to be good, the fingerprint may not perceptibly deteriorate its quality:

Definition 3 (Goodness). Goodness *is a predicate* Good : $\mathcal{M}^2 \to \{\text{true},$ $\text{false}\}$ *over two messages* $M_1, M_2 \in \mathcal{M}$ *that evaluates their perceptual difference. A fingerprinted copy* $M^{(i)}$ *is called* good *if its perceptual difference to the original content* M *is below a perceptibility threshold. We denote this with* $\text{Good}(M^{(i)}, M) = \text{true}$. *Otherwise, the copy is called* bad.

Definition 4 (Correctness). *Let* $p^{\text{bad}} \ll 1$ *be the maximum allowed probability of a bad copy. A fingercasting scheme is* correct *if the probability for a non-revoked receiver to obtain a bad copy* $M^{(i)}$ *of the content* M *is at most* p^{bad}, *where the probability is taken over all coin tosses of the setup and encryption algorithm:*

$$\forall M \in \mathcal{M}, \forall u_i \in \mathcal{U} \setminus \mathcal{R}: \quad \Pr\left[\text{Good}(M, M^{(i)}) = \text{false}\right] \leq p^{\text{bad}}$$

The SSW scheme of [15] uses the goodness predicate $||M^{(i)} - M|| \leq \sqrt{n'}\delta$, where n' is the number of content coefficients and δ a goodness criterion.

All relevant BE schemes provide IND-CCA1 security [6,7,8], which is a stronger notion than IND-CPA security. As we aim to achieve at least IND-CPA security, the remaining requirements only relate to the Chameleon scheme $\mathcal{CE}$.

We define IND-CPA security of $\mathcal{CE}$ by a game between an IND-CPA adversary $\mathcal{A}$ and a challenger $\mathcal{C}$: The challenger runs $(MT, TF, t) \leftarrow \text{KeyGenCE}(N, 1^{\lambda'}, par_{\text{CE}})$, generates a secret random session key k^{sess} and sends (MT, TF, t) to $\mathcal{A}$. $\mathcal{A}$ outputs two content items $M_0, M_1 \in \mathcal{M}$ on which it wishes to be challenged. $\mathcal{C}$ picks a random bit $b \xleftarrow{R} \{0, 1\}$ and sends the challenge ciphertext $C_b \leftarrow \text{EncCE}(MT, k^{\text{sess}}, M_b)$ to $\mathcal{A}$. Finally, $\mathcal{A}$ outputs a guess b' and wins if $b' = b$. We define the advantage of $\mathcal{A}$ against $\mathcal{CE}$ as $\text{Adv}_{\mathcal{A}, \mathcal{CE}}^{\text{ind-cpa}}(\lambda') := |\Pr[b' = 0|b = 0] - \Pr[b' = 0|b = 1]|$. For further details on security notions we refer to [25].

Definition 5 (IND-CPA security). *A Chameleon scheme* $\mathcal{CE}$ *is* IND-CPA *secure if for every probabilistic polynomial-time* IND-CPA *adversary* $\mathcal{A}$ *we have that* $\text{Adv}_{\mathcal{A}, \mathcal{CE}}^{\text{ind-cpa}}(\lambda')$ *is a negligible function.*

We note that in Definition 5, the adversary is not an outsider or third party, but an insider in possession of the master table (not only a receiver table). Nevertheless, the adversary should have a negligible advantage in distinguishing the ciphertexts of two messages of his choice as long as the session key remains secret.

Collusion resistance is defined by the following game between an adversarial coalition $\mathcal{A} \subseteq \mathcal{U} \setminus \mathcal{R}$ and a challenger $\mathcal{C}$: The challenger runs KeyGenCE on parameters $(N, 1^{\lambda'}, par_{\text{CE}})$, generates a ciphertext $C \leftarrow \text{EncCE}(MT, k^{\text{sess}}, M)$, and gives $\mathcal{A}$ the receiver tables $RT^{(i)}$ of all coalition members as well as the session key k^{sess}. Then $\mathcal{A}$ outputs a document copy M^* and wins if for all coalition members the detection algorithm fails (false negative):

Definition 6 (Collusion resistance). *Let* DetectFP *be the fingerprint detection algorithm of the fingerprinting scheme that a Chameleon scheme* $\mathcal{CE}$ *instantiates. Then* $\mathcal{CE}$ *is* (q, p^{neg})*-collusion-resistant if for every probabilistic polynomial-time adversarial coalition* $\mathcal{A}$ *of at most* $q := |\mathcal{A}|$ *colluders we have that*

$$\Pr\left[\mathsf{Good}(M^*, M)\mathsf{=true}, \forall u_i \in \mathcal{A} : \mathsf{DetectFP}(M, M^*, CF^{(i)}, t)\mathsf{=false}\right] \leq p^{\mathsf{neg}},$$

where the false negative probability is taken over the coin tosses of the setup algorithm, of the adversarial coalition $\mathcal{A}$*, and of the session key* k^{sess}*.*

Note that 1-collusion resistance is also called robustness. Frame-proofness is similar to collusion resistance, but $\mathcal{A}$ wins the game if the detection algorithm accuses an innocent user (false positive).

Definition 7 (Frame-proofness). *Let* DetectFP *be the fingerprint detection algorithm of the fingerprinting scheme that a Chameleon scheme* $\mathcal{CE}$ *instantiates. Then* $\mathcal{CE}$ *is* (q, p^{pos})*-frame-proof if for every probabilistic polynomial-time adversarial coalition* $\mathcal{A}$ *of at most* $q := |\mathcal{A}|$ *colluders we have that*

$$\Pr\left[\mathsf{Good}(M^*, M)\mathsf{=true}, \exists u_i \notin \mathcal{A} : \mathsf{DetectFP}(M, M^*, CF^{(i)}, t)\mathsf{=true}\right] \leq p^{\mathsf{pos}},$$

where the false positive probability is taken over the coin tosses of the setup algorithm, of the adversarial coalition $\mathcal{A}$*, and of the session key* k^{sess}*.*

In Definitions 6 and 7, the adversarial coalition again consists of insiders in possession of their receiver tables and the session key. Nevertheless, the coalition should have a well-defined and small chance of creating a plaintext copy that incriminates none of the coalition members (collusion resistance) or an innocent user outside the coalition (frame-proofness).

4 Proposed Solution

4.1 High-Level Overview of the Proposed Fingercasting Scheme

To fingercast content, the center uses the BE scheme to send a fresh session key to each non-revoked receiver. This session key initializes a pseudo-random sequence generator. The resulting pseudo-random sequence represents a sequence of addresses in the master table of our new Chameleon scheme. The center encrypts the content with the master table entries to which the addresses refer. Each receiver has a unique receiver table that differs only slightly from the master table. During decryption, these slight differences in the receiver table lead to slight, but characteristic differences in the content copy.

Interaction Details. We divide this approach into the same five steps that we have seen for Chameleon schemes in Section 3.3. First, the *key generation* algorithm of the fingercasting scheme consists of the key generations algorithms of the two underlying schemes KeyGenBE and KeyGenCE. The center's master key thus consists of MK, MT and TF. Second, the same observation holds for the *key extraction* algorithm of the fingercasting scheme. It consists of the respective algorithms in the two underlying schemes KeyExtrBE and KeyExtrCE. The secret key of receiver u_i therefore has two elements: $SK^{(i)}$ and $RT^{(i)}$.

Third, the *encryption* algorithm defines how we interlock the two underlying schemes. To encrypt, the center generates a fresh and random session key $k^{\text{sess}} \xleftarrow{R} \{0,1\}^\lambda$. This session key is broadcasted to the non-revoked receivers using the BE scheme: $C_{\text{BE}} \leftarrow \text{EncBE}(MK, \mathcal{R}, k^{\text{sess}})$. Subsequently, the center uses k^{sess} to determine addresses in the master table MT of the Chameleon scheme and encrypts with the corresponding entries: $C_{\text{CE}} \leftarrow \text{EncCE}(MT, k^{\text{sess}}, M)$. The ciphertext of the fingercasting scheme thus has two elements C_{BE} and C_{CE}.

Fourth, the *decryption* algorithm inverts the encryption algorithm with unnoticeable, but characteristic errors. First of all, each non-revoked receiver u_i recovers the correct session key: $k^{\text{sess}} \leftarrow \text{DecBE}(i, SK^{(i)}, C_{\text{BE}})$. Therefore, u_i can recalculate the PRS and the correct addresses in receiver table $RT^{(i)}$. However, this receiver table is slightly different from the master table. Therefore, u_i obtains a fingerprinted copy $M^{(i)}$ that is slightly different from the original content: $M^{(i)} \leftarrow \text{DecCE}(RT^{(i)}, k^{\text{sess}}, C_{\text{CE}})$. Last, the *fingerprint detection* algorithm of the fingercasting scheme is identical to that of the underlying fingerprinting scheme.

4.2   A New Chameleon Scheme

Up to now, we have focused on the straightforward aspects of our approach; we have neglected the intrinsic difficulties and the impact of the requirements on the Chameleon scheme. In the sequel, we will show a specific Chameleon scheme that fulfills all of them. We design it in such a way that its content fingerprints can emulate any additive fingerprinting scheme, which we later instantiate with the SSW scheme as proof of concept.

Key Generation. To define this algorithm, we need to determine how the center generates the master table MT and the table fingerprints TF. To generate MT, the center chooses L table entries at random from the interval $[0, z]$ with independent uniform distribution: $mt_\alpha \xleftarrow{R} [0, z]$ for all $\alpha \in \{1, \ldots, L\}$. As the table entries will be addressed with bit words, we select $L = 2^l$ such that l indicates the number of bits needed to define the binary address of an entry in the table. The center thus obtains the master table $MT := (mt_1, mt_2, \ldots, mt_L)$.

To generate the table fingerprints $TF := (TF^{(1)}, \ldots, TF^{(N)})$, the center selects for each receiver u_i and each master table entry mt_α a fingerprint coefficient in order to disturb the original entry. Specifically, each fingerprint coefficient $tf_\alpha^{(i)}$ of table fingerprint $TF^{(i)}$ is independently distributed according to the probability distribution ProDis of the additive fingerprinting scheme, but scaled down with an attenuation factor $f \in \mathbb{R}$, $f \geq 1$:

$$tf_\alpha^{(i)} \leftarrow 1/f \cdot \text{ProDis}(par_{\text{FP}}) \tag{1}$$

Key Extraction. After the probabilistic key generation algorithm we now describe the deterministic key extraction algorithm. The center processes table

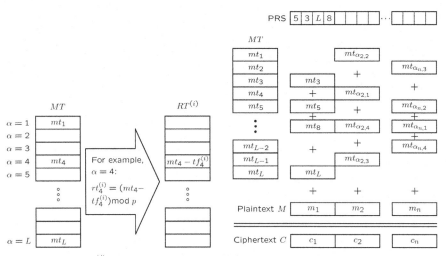

(a) To derive $RT^{(i)}$ from MT, the center subtracts the L fingerprint coefficients $tf_\alpha^{(i)}$ at address α for all $\alpha \in \{1, \ldots, L\}$.

(b) To derive ciphertext C from plaintext M, the center uses the session key to generate a PRS. It then adds the addressed master table entries to the plaintext.

Fig. 1. Receiver table derivation and ciphertext calculation

fingerprint $TF^{(i)} := (tf_1^{(i)}, \ldots, tf_L^{(i)})$ of receiver u_i as follows: The center subtracts each fingerprint coefficient in $TF^{(i)}$ from the corresponding master table entry to obtain the receiver table entry, which we illustrate in Fig. 1(a):

$$\forall \alpha \in \{1, \ldots, L\}: \quad rt_\alpha^{(i)} \leftarrow mt_\alpha - tf_\alpha^{(i)} \bmod p \qquad (2)$$

Remark 1. The modulo operator allows only integer values to be added. However, the master table, the table fingerprints and the content coefficients are based on real numbers with finite precision. We solve this ostensible contradiction by scaling the real values to the integer domain by an appropriate scaling factor ρ, possibly ignoring further decimal digits. ρ must be chosen large enough to allow a computation in the integer domain with a sufficiently high precision. We implicitly assume this scaling to the integer domain whenever real values are used. For example, with real-valued variables $rt^{(i)}$, mt, and $tf^{(i)}$ the operation $rt^{(i)} \leftarrow (mt - tf^{(i)}) \bmod p$ actually stands for $\rho \cdot rt^{(i)} \leftarrow (\rho \cdot mt - \rho \cdot tf^{(i)}) \bmod p$. The group order $p := \lceil \rho \cdot z \rceil + 1$ is defined by the content space $[0, z]$ (see Section 3.2) and the scaling factor ρ.

Encryption. Fig. 1(b) gives an overview of the encryption algorithm. The session key k^{sess} is used as the seed of a PRSG with expansion function $\mathsf{len}(|k^{\mathsf{sess}}|) \geq n \cdot s \cdot l$, where parameter s will be specified below. To give a practical example for a PRSG, k^{sess} may serve as the key for a conventional block cipher, e.g., AES or triple DES,[3] in output feedback mode. Each block of l bits of the pseudo-random sequence is interpreted as an address β in the master table MT. For each coefficient of the plaintext, the center uses s addresses that define s entries of the master table. In total, the center obtains $n \cdot s$ addresses that we denote with $\beta_{j,k}$, where j is the coefficient index, k the address index, and $\mathsf{Extract}_i$ extracts the i-th block of length l from its input string:

$$\forall j \in \{1, \dots, n\}, \; \forall k \in \{1, \dots, s\} : \quad \beta_{j,k} \leftarrow \mathsf{Extract}_{(j-1)s+k}(\mathsf{G}(k^{\mathsf{sess}})) \quad (3)$$

For each content coefficient, the center adds the s master table entries modulo the group order. In Fig. 1(b), we illustrate the case $s = 4$, which is the design choice in the original Chameleon cipher. The j-th coefficient c_j of the ciphertext C is calculated as

$$\forall j \in \{1, \dots, n\} : \quad c_j \leftarrow \left(m_j + \sum_{k=1}^{s} mt_{\beta_{j,k}} \right) \bmod p, \quad (4)$$

where $mt_{\beta_{j,k}}$ denotes the master table entry referenced by address $\beta_{j,k}$ from (3).

Decryption. The decryption algorithm proceeds in the same way as the encryption algorithm with two exceptions. First, the receiver has to use its receiver table $RT^{(i)}$ instead of MT. Second, the addition is replaced by subtraction. The j-th coefficient $m_j^{(i)}$ of the plaintext copy $M^{(i)}$ of receiver u_i is thus calculated as

$$m_j^{(i)} \leftarrow \left(c_j - \sum_{k=1}^{s} rt_{\beta_{j,k}}^{(i)} \right) \bmod p, \quad (5)$$

where $rt_{\beta_{j,k}}^{(i)}$ denotes the receiver table entry of receiver u_i referenced by address $\beta_{j,k}$ generated in (3). As the receiver table $RT^{(i)}$ slightly differs from the master table MT, the plaintext copy $M^{(i)}$ obtained by receiver u_i slightly differs from the original plaintext M. By appropriately choosing the attenuation factor f in (1), the distortion of $M^{(i)}$ with respect to M is the same as that of the instantiated fingerprinting scheme and goodness is preserved (see Section 4.3).

Fingerprint Detection. When the center detects an illegal copy $M^* = (m_1^*, \dots, m_n^*)$ of content M, it tries to identify the receivers that participated in the generation of M^*. To do so, the center verifies whether the fingerprint of a suspect receiver u_i is present in M^*. Obviously, the fingerprint is unlikely to appear in its original form; an adversary may have modified it by applying common attacks such as resampling, requantization, compression, cropping, and rotation. Furthermore, the adversary may have applied an arbitrary combination of these known attacks and other yet unknown attacks. Finally, an adversarial coalition may have colluded and created M^* using several different copies of M.

The fingerprint detection algorithm is identical to that of the underlying fingerprinting scheme: $dec \leftarrow \mathsf{DetectFP}(M, M^*, CF^{(i)}, t)$. In order to properly scale

---

[3] Advanced Encryption Standard [26] and Data Encryption Standard [27].

the content fingerprint, we need to select the attenuation factor f in (1). We choose it such that the addition of s attenuated fingerprint coefficients generates a random variable that follows ProDis *without* attenuation (for an example see Section 4.3). In order to verify whether the table fingerprint $TF^{(i)}$ of receiver u_i left traces in M^*, DetectFP calculates the similarity between the detected content fingerprint CF^* with coefficients $cf_j^* := m_j^* - m_j$ and the content fingerprint $CF^{(i)}$ in u_i's copy $M^{(i)}$ with

$$cf_j^{(i)} := m_j^{(i)} - m_j \overset{(4),(5)}{=} \sum_{k=1}^{s} \left(mt_{\beta_{j,k}} - rt_{\beta_{j,k}}^{(i)} \right) \overset{(2)}{=} \sum_{k=1}^{s} tf_{\beta_{j,k}}^{(i)}, \tag{6}$$

where $tf_{\beta_{j,k}}^{(i)}$ is the fingerprint coefficient that fingerprinted receiver table $RT^{(i)}$ at address $\alpha = \beta_{j,k}$ in (2). If the similarity is above threshold t, the center declares u_i guilty. Note that the calculation of CF^* necessitates the original content M, whereas the calculation of $CF^{(i)}$ relies on the session key k^{sess} and the table fingerprint $TF^{(i)}$; the scheme is thus non-blind in its current version. However, we assume it is possible to design an extended scheme with a blind detection algorithm. If instantiated with Spread Spectrum Watermarking, the watermark is often robust enough to be detected even in the absence of the original content.

The same algorithm applies to detection of fingerprints in illegal copies of receiver tables. Their fingerprints have the same construction and statistical properties, where the attenuated amplitude of the fingerprint coefficients in (1) is compensated by a higher number of coefficients, as the relation $L/f \approx n$ holds for practical parameter choices (see Section 5.1).

When the center detects the fingerprint of a certain user in an illegal content copy or an illegal receiver table, there are two potential countermeasures with different security and performance tradeoffs. One is to simply revoke the user in the BE scheme such that the user's BE decryption key becomes useless and no longer grants access to the session key. However, the user's receiver table still allows to decrypt content if yet another user illegally shares the session key. In an Internet age, this is a valid threat as two illegal users may collude such that one user publishes the receiver table (and gets caught) and the other user anonymously publishes the session keys (and doesn't get caught). Nevertheless, we stress that this weakness, namely the non-traceability of session keys, is common to all revocation BE schemes because the session key is identical for all users and therefore does not allow tracing.[4]

In order to avoid this weakness, the other potential countermeasure is to not only revoke the user whose receiver table was illegally shared, but also renew the master table and redistribute the new receiver tables. If the broadcast channel has enough spare bandwidth, the center can broadcast the receiver tables individually to all receivers in off-peak periods, i.e., when the channel's bandwidth

---

[4] The common assumption for revocation BE schemes is that it is difficult to share the session key anonymously on a large scale without being caught. Even if key sharing may be possible on a small scale, e.g., among family and friends, the main goal is to allow revocation of a user that shared the decryption key or session keys and got caught, no matter by which means of technical or legal tracing.

is not fully used for regular transmission. The relevant BE schemes [6,7,8] allow to encrypt each receiver table individually for the corresponding receiver such that only this receiver can decrypt and obtain access.[5] If the broadcast channel's bandwidth is too low, then the receiver tables need to be redistributed as in the initial setup phase, e.g., via smartcards.

Parameter Selection. The new Chameleon scheme has two major parameters L and s that allow a trade-off between the size of $RT^{(i)}$, which u_i has to store, and the computation cost, which grows linearly with the number s of addresses per content coefficient in (4). By increasing L, we can decrease s in order to replace computation cost with storage size. Further details follow in Section 5.1.

4.3   Instantiation with Spread Spectrum Watermarking

In this section, we instantiate the fingerprinting scheme with the SSW scheme of [15] and thereby inherit its collusion resistance and frame-proofness. Let the center choose the SSW scheme's parameters $par_{\mathsf{FP}} = (\delta, p^{\mathsf{bad}}, p^{\mathsf{pos}})$, which allows to calculate a standard deviation σ' and a threshold t via two functions $f_{\sigma'}(N, n', \delta, p^{\mathsf{bad}})$ and $f_t(\sigma', N, p^{\mathsf{pos}})$ defined in [15]. The probability distribution of the SSW scheme is then $\mathsf{ProDis} = \mathsf{N}(0, \sigma')$. We set $f = s$ because then $1/f \cdot \mathsf{N}(0, \sigma')$ in (1) is still a normal distribution with mean 0 and standard deviation $1/\sqrt{s} \cdot \sigma'$, and adding s of those variables in (4) and (5) leads to the required random variable with standard deviation σ'. It remains to define the similarity measure for the detection algorithm $dec \leftarrow \mathsf{DetectFP}(M, M^*, CF^{(i)}, t)$, which [15] defines as:

$$dec = \mathtt{true} \quad \text{if} \quad \frac{CF^* \cdot CF^{(i)}}{||CF^*||} > t$$

We call an instantiation *exact* if it achieves the same statistical properties as the fingerprinting scheme that it instantiates. Theorem 2 below states that the above choice is an exact instantiation of the SSW scheme.

Theorem 2. *Let σ' and σ be the standard deviations of the SSW scheme and the Chameleon scheme instantiated with SSW, respectively, and n' and n be their number of content coefficients. Then the following mapping between both schemes is an exact instantiation:*

$$\sigma' = \sqrt{s} \cdot \sigma \ (\Leftrightarrow f = s) \qquad and \qquad n' = n$$

Towards the proof of Theorem 2. We prove an even stronger result than Theorem 2. In addition to the exactness of the instantiation, we also prove that it is optimal to fingerprint *every* entry of the receiver tables. To do so, we first formulate Lemmata 1–4 and then describe why they imply Theorem 2. For

---

[5] In all of these schemes, the center shares with each user an individual secret, which they can use for regular symmetric encryption.

the Lemmata, we introduce a parameter $F \in \{1, 2, \ldots, L\}$ that describes the number of receiver table entries that obtain a fingerprint coefficient $tf_\alpha^{(i)}$ in (2). The position of the F fingerprinted entries in the receiver table is selected with uniform distribution. We show that the choice $F = L$ is optimal in the sense that the resulting instantiation is exact.

The difficulty in analyzing the SSW instantiation is that each content coefficient is not only fingerprinted with a single fingerprint coefficient as in SSW, but with up to s such variables as can be seen from (6). Note that for $F < L$ some receiver table entries do not receive a fingerprint coefficient and are therefore identical to the master table entry. In order to analyze the statistical properties of the resulting fingerprint, we will need to calculate the expectation and variance of two parameters that link the instantiation to the original SSW scheme.

The first parameter is the number N^{fp} of fingerprint coefficients $tf^{(i)}$ that are added to a content coefficient m_j by using the receiver table $RT^{(i)}$ in (5) instead of the master table MT in (4). In SSW, N^{fp} has the constant value 1, i.e., a content fingerprint consists of one fingerprint coefficient per content coefficient, whereas in our scheme N^{fp} varies between 0 and s as shown in (6). If only F of the L receiver table entries have been fingerprinted, then $tf^{(i)} = 0$ for the remaining $L - F$ entries.

The second parameter is the number of content coefficients that carry a detectable content fingerprint. In SSW, this number has the constant value n', i.e., every coefficient carries a fingerprint with fixed standard deviation, whereas in our scheme, some of the n coefficients may happen to receive no or only few fingerprint coefficients $tf^{(i)}$. Specifically, this happens when the receiver table entry $rt_{\beta_{j,k}}^{(i)}$ of (5) did not receive a fingerprint coefficient in (2) for $F < L$. The next lemma gives the number of normally distributed table fingerprint coefficients that our scheme adds to a content coefficient. This number is a random variable characterized by its expectation and standard variance.

We prove the lemmata under the *uniform sequence assumption*, i.e., the sequence used to select the addresses from the master table has independent uniform distribution. We stress that we only use it to find the optimal mapping with SSW; security and collusion resistance of the proposed scheme do *not* rely on this assumption for the final choice of parameters (see the end of this section).[6]

Lemma 1. *Let N^{fp} be the random variable counting the number of fingerprinted receiver table entries with which a coefficient $m_j^{(i)}$ of copy $M^{(i)}$ is fingerprinted. Then the probability of obtaining $k \in \{0, \ldots, s\}$ fingerprinted entries is*

$$\mathsf{Pr}\left[N^{\mathsf{fp}} = k\right] = \binom{s}{k} (\frac{F}{L})^k (1 - \frac{F}{L})^{s-k}$$

The expectation and the variance of N^{fp} are

$$\mathsf{E}(N^{\mathsf{fp}}) = s\frac{F}{L} \quad and \quad \sigma_{N^{\mathsf{fp}}}^2 := \mathsf{E}([N^{\mathsf{fp}} - \mathsf{E}(N^{\mathsf{fp}})]^2) = s\frac{F}{L}(1 - \frac{F}{L}).$$

---

[6] Note that even if this was not the case, we can show that the adversary's advantage is still negligible by a simple reduction argument.

Proof. During decryption, the receiver subtracts s receiver table entries $rt_\alpha^{(i)}$ from the ciphertext coefficient using (5). Each entry $rt_\alpha^{(i)}$ is either fingerprinted or not. Under the uniform sequence assumption, the addresses of the subtracted entries $rt_\alpha^{(i)}$ have independent uniform distribution. In addition, the F fingerprinted entries are distributed over $RT^{(i)}$ with independent uniform distribution. Therefore, the probability that a single address $\alpha = \beta_{j,k}$ in (5) points to a fingerprinted receiver table entry $rt_\alpha^{(i)}$ is F/L, which is the number of fingerprinted receiver table entries divided by the total number of entries. As the underlying experiment is a sequence of s consecutive yes-no experiments with success probability F/L, it follows that N^{fp} has binomial distribution. This implies the probability, the expectation, and the variance.

Lemma 1 allows us to determine how many fingerprint coefficients we can expect in each content coefficient and how the number of such fingerprint coefficients varies. The next question is what kind of random variable results from adding N^{fp} fingerprint coefficients.

Lemma 2. *By adding a number N^{fp} of independent $\mathsf{N}(0, \sigma)$-distributed fingerprint coefficients, the resulting random variable has normal distribution with mean 0 and standard deviation $\sqrt{N^{\mathsf{fp}}}\sigma$.*

Proof. Each fingerprint coefficient is independently distributed according to the normal distribution $\mathsf{N}(0, \sigma)$. When two independent and normally distributed random variables are added, the resulting random variable is also normally distributed, while the means and the variances add up. Due to linearity, the resulting standard deviation for N^{fp} random variables is $\sqrt{N^{\mathsf{fp}}\sigma^2} = \sqrt{N^{\mathsf{fp}}}\sigma$.

In order to fingerprint the content coefficients with the same standard deviation σ' as in the SSW scheme, the natural choice is to choose σ such that $\sqrt{\mathsf{E}(N^{\mathsf{fp}})}\sigma = \sigma'$. The remaining question is how many content coefficients are actually fingerprinted; note that due to the randomness of N^{fp}, some content coefficients may receive more fingerprint coefficients than others. We determine the expected number of fingerprinted content coefficients in the next two lemmata, while we leave it open how many fingerprint coefficients are needed for detection:

Lemma 3. *Let $N_{\min}^{\mathsf{fp}} \in \{1, \ldots, s\}$ be the minimum number of table fingerprint coefficients needed to obtain a detectable fingerprint in content coefficient $m_j^{(i)}$. Then the probability p^{fing} that coefficient $m_j^{(i)}$ of copy $M^{(i)}$ obtains at least $N_{\min}^{\mathsf{fp}}$ fingerprint coefficients is*

$$p^{\mathsf{fing}} = \sum_{k=N_{\min}^{\mathsf{fp}}}^{s} \binom{s}{k} \left(\frac{F}{L}\right)^k \left(1 - \frac{F}{L}\right)^{s-k}$$

Proof. The lemma is a corollary of Lemma 1 by adding the probabilities of all events whose value of N^{fp} is greater than or equal to $N_{\min}^{\mathsf{fp}}$.

Lemma 4. *Let $N^{\text{fing}} \in \{0, \ldots, n\}$ be the random variable counting the number of fingerprinted coefficients. Then the expectation of N^{fing} is*

$$\mathsf{E}(N^{\text{fing}}) = \sum_{j=0}^{n} j \binom{n}{j} (p^{\text{fing}})^j (1 - p^{\text{fing}})^{n-j} = np^{\text{fing}}$$

Proof. The lemma follows from the fact that N^{fing} has binomial distribution with success probability p^{fing} and n experiments.

Given Lemmata 1–4 we can derive some of the parameters in our scheme from SSW. Suppose that the center has already selected the parameters of the SSW scheme such that the requirements on the number of receivers and collusion resistance are met. This includes the choice of N, n', and $par_{\text{FP}} = par_{\text{CE}} := (\delta, p^{\text{bad}}, p^{\text{pos}})$; it allows to derive σ' and t of SSW based on the functions $\mathsf{f}_{\sigma'}(N, n', \delta, p^{\text{bad}})$ and $\mathsf{f}_t(\sigma', N, p^{\text{pos}})$, which are defined in [15].

Based on the center's selection, we can derive the parameters n, F/L, and $\sqrt{s} \cdot \sigma$ in our Chameleon scheme as follows. Our first aim is to achieve the same expected standard deviation in the content coefficients of our scheme as in SSW, i.e., $\sigma' = \sqrt{\mathsf{E}(N^{\text{fp}})} \cdot \sigma$, which by Lemma 1 leads to $\sigma' = \sqrt{sF/L} \cdot \sigma$. Our second aim is to minimize the variance of N^{fp} in order to have $N^{\text{fp}} = \mathsf{E}(N^{\text{fp}})$ not only on average, but for as many content coefficients as possible, where $N^{\text{fp}} = \mathsf{E}(N^{\text{fp}})$ implies that the content coefficient in our scheme obtains a fingerprint with the same statistical properties as in SSW. The two minima of $\sigma_{N^{\text{fp}}}^2 = s \cdot F/L \cdot (1 - F/L)$ are $F/L = 0$ and $F/L = 1$, of which only the second is meaningful. $F/L = 1$ or $F = L$ is the case where all entries of the master table are fingerprinted. As this optimum case leads to a variance of $\sigma_{N^{\text{fp}}}^2 = 0$ and $N^{\text{fp}} = s$, the content coefficients of our scheme and SSW have the same statistical properties. This proves Theorem 2 and the claim that all tables entries should be fingerprinted.

With $F/L = 1$ and $\sigma' = \sqrt{s} \cdot \sigma$, we obtain $\Pr\left[N^{\text{fp}} = s\right] = 1$ by Lemma 1 and $p^{\text{fing}} = 1$ by Lemma 3. Finally, we conclude that $\mathsf{E}(N^{\text{fing}}) = n \cdot p^{\text{fing}} = n$ by Lemma 4 and set $\mathsf{E}(N^{\text{fing}}) = n = n'$. We stress that the equalities hold even if we replace the uniform sequence with a pseudo-random sequence; for $F = L$ the equations $N^{\text{fp}} = s$ and $N^{\text{fing}} = n$ are obviously independent of the uniform distribution of the sequence of addresses in the master table.

We note that the number s of addresses per content coefficient, introduced in (4), is still undetermined and may be chosen according to the security requirements (see Section 4.4).

4.4 Analysis

Correctness, Collusion Resistance and Frame-Proofness. Correctness follows from the correctness of the two underlying schemes, i.e., the BE scheme and the Chameleon scheme. Correctness of the Chameleon scheme follows from the correctness of the underlying fingerprinting scheme, which we can instantiate exactly by properly choosing the scaling factor in (1) and thus making the content fingerprint of (6) identical to a fingerprint of the instantiated fingerprinting scheme. Collusion resistance and frame-proofness of content *and* receiver tables follows from the collusion resistance and frame-proofness of the instantiated fingerprinting scheme.

The mapping in Section 4.3 is an exact instantiation of the SSW scheme and therefore inherits its collusion resistance and frame-proofness (see Theorem 1). We note that the proof of Theorem 1, which appears in [15], covers both collusion resistance *and* frame-proofness, although the original text of the theorem only seems to cover collusion resistance. Collusion resistance, related to false negatives, is shown in [15, Section 3.4], whereas frame-proofness, related to false positives, is shown in [15, Section 3.2].

IND-CPA Security. We reduce the security of our Chameleon scheme to that of the PRSG with which it is instantiated. In order to prove IND-CPA security, we prove that the key stream produced by the Chameleon scheme is pseudo-random (see Definition 1). IND-CPA security of the proposed scheme follows by a simple reduction argument (see [28, Section 5.3.1]). To further strengthen the proof, we assume that the adversary is in possession of the master table and all receiver tables, although in practice the adversary only has one or several receiver tables.

By scaling the real values of the content coefficients to the integer domain (see Remark 1), we obtain a plaintext symbol space $\mathcal{P}$ with a cardinality Z defined by the content and the scaling factor ρ. In the remainder of this section we assume that the plaintext symbol space $\mathcal{P}$ and the key symbol space $\mathcal{K}$ are equal to $\{0, 1, \ldots, Z - 1\}$. We make this assumption to simplify our notation, but stress that this is no restriction, as there is a one-to-one mapping between the actual plaintext symbol space $[0, z]$ and the scaled space $\{0, 1, \ldots, Z - 1\}$, which enumerates the elements of $[0, z]$ starting from 0.[7] In the sequel, by *key symbols* we mean the elements of $\mathcal{K}$. We also note that the obvious choice for the group order p is the size of the symbol space: $p = |\mathcal{K}| = Z$. This ensures identical size of plaintext and ciphertext space.

The proof is divided into 4 major steps. First, we show the properties of the random variable that results from a single draw from the master table (Lemma 5). Second, we define these properties as the starting point of an iteration on the number s of draws from the master table (Definition 8). Third, we prove that the random variable that results from adding randomly drawn master table entries improves with every draw, where improving means being statistically closer to a truly random variable (Lemma 6). Last, we prove the pseudo-randomness of the Chameleon scheme's key stream (Theorem 3).

Lemma 5. *Let* $\Pr\left[X^{(1)} = x\right]$ *denote the probability of drawing the key symbol* $x \in \mathcal{K}$ *in a single draw from master table* MT. *Let* $\eta_k \in \{0, 1, \ldots, L\}$ *denote the number of times that key symbol* $x_k \in \mathcal{K}$ *appears in* MT. *When we select a master table entry at a random address with uniform distribution, then the probability of obtaining key symbol* $x_k \in \mathcal{K}$ *is* $p_k := \Pr\left[X^{(1)} = x_k\right] = \frac{\eta_k}{L}$.

---

[7] Note that $[0, z]$ consists of real numbers with finite precision. As pointed out in Remark 1 these real numbers are mapped to integers by applying a scaling factor ρ.

Proof. There are L entries in the master table. Due to the uniform distribution of the selected address, each master table entry has the same probability of being selected. Therefore, the probability of a specific key symbol $x_k \in \mathcal{K}$ being selected is the number η_k of occurrences of x_k in the master table divided by the total number L of master table entries.

For a single draw from the master table, the resulting random variable thus only depends on the number of occurrences of the key symbols within the master table. As the master table entries are generated with uniform distribution, the frequencies are unlikely to be identical for each key symbol, leading to a non-uniform and therefore insecure distribution $\mathsf{Pr}\left[X^{(1)}\right]$.

Definition 8 (Strong convergence). *Let U be a random variable uniformly distributed over the key symbol space. Let the statistical quality $SQ^{(1)}$ of MT be the statistical difference between $X^{(1)}$ and U: $SQ^{(1)} := \frac{1}{2}\sum_{k=0}^{Z-1}\left|p_k - \frac{1}{Z}\right|$. We call the master table* strongly converging *if $2SQ^{(1)} \leq d$ for some $d \in \mathbb{R}$ such that $d < 1$.*

The statistical quality $SQ^{(1)}$ is thus a measure for the initial suitability of the master table for generating a uniform distribution. The next lemma is the main result of the security analysis; it proves that the statistical quality $SQ^{(s)}$ gets better with every of the s draws.

Lemma 6. *Let U be a random variable uniformly distributed over the key symbol space. Let MT be a strongly converging master table. Let X_k denote the k-th draw from MT and $X^{(s)}$ the random variable resulting from s independent uniformly distributed draws added modulo Z: $X^{(s)} := \sum_{k=1}^{s} X_k \bmod Z$. Then the statistical difference $SQ^{(s)}$ between $X^{(s)}$ and U is a negligible function with an upper bound of $\frac{1}{2}d^s$.*

Proof. The proof is by induction. For all $k \in \mathcal{K}$, let $p_k^{(i)} := \mathsf{Pr}\left[X^{(i)} = k\right]$ denote the probability of the event that in the i-th iteration the random variable $X^{(i)}$ takes the value of key symbol k. Represent this probability with an additive error $e_k^{(i)}$ such that $p_k^{(i)} = \frac{1}{Z}(1 + e_k^{(i)})$. Due to $\sum_{k=0}^{Z-1} p_k^{(i)} = 1$, we obtain $\sum_{k=0}^{Z-1} e_k^{(i)} = 0$. The induction start is trivially fulfilled by every strongly converging master table: $SQ^{(1)} \leq \frac{1}{2}d$. As the induction hypothesis, we have $SQ^{(i)} \leq \frac{1}{2}d^i$, where $SQ^{(i)} := \frac{1}{2}\sum_{k=0}^{Z-1}\left|p_k^{(i)} - \frac{1}{Z}\right| = \frac{1}{2Z}\sum_{k=0}^{Z-1}\left|e_k^{(i)}\right|$. The induction claim is $SQ^{(i+1)} \leq \frac{1}{2}d^{i+1}$. The induction proof follows: Iteration $i+1$ is defined as $X^{(i+1)} := \sum_{k=1}^{i+1} X_k \bmod Z$, which is equal to $X^{(i+1)} = X^{(i)} + X_{i+1} \bmod Z$, where X_{i+1} is just a single draw with the probabilities p_k from Lemma 5 and error representation $p_k = \frac{1}{Z}(1 + e_k)$ such that $\sum_{k=0}^{Z-1} e_k = 0$. Therefore, we obtain for all $k \in \mathcal{K}$ that

$$\mathsf{Pr}\left[X^{(i+1)} = k\right] = \sum_{j=0}^{Z-1} \mathsf{Pr}\left[X^{(i)} = j\right] \cdot \mathsf{Pr}\left[X_{i+1} = (k-j) \bmod Z\right]$$

$$= \sum_{j=0}^{Z-1} p_j^{(i)} p_{(k-j) \bmod Z} = \frac{1}{Z^2} \sum_{j=0}^{Z-1} (1 + e_j^{(i)})(1 + e_{(k-j) \bmod Z})$$

$$= \frac{1}{Z^2} \left(\underbrace{\sum_{j=0}^{Z-1} 1 + \underbrace{\sum_{j=0}^{Z-1} e_j^{(i)}}_{=0} + \underbrace{\sum_{j=0}^{Z-1} e_{(k-j) \bmod Z}}_{=0} + \sum_{j=0}^{Z-1} e_j^{(i)} e_{(k-j) \bmod Z}} \right)$$

$$= \frac{1}{Z} + \frac{1}{Z^2} \sum_{j=0}^{Z-1} e_j^{(i)} e_{(k-j) \bmod Z}$$

The upper bound for the statistical difference in iteration $i + 1$ is

$$SQ^{(i+1)} := \frac{1}{2} \sum_{k=0}^{Z-1} \left| \Pr\left[X^{(i+1)} = k \right] - \frac{1}{Z} \right| = \frac{1}{2} \sum_{k=0}^{Z-1} \left| \frac{1}{Z^2} \sum_{j=0}^{Z-1} e_j^{(i)} e_{(k-j) \bmod Z} \right|$$

$$\leq \frac{1}{2Z^2} \left(\sum_{k=0}^{Z-1} \left| e_k^{(i)} \right| \right) \left(\sum_{k=0}^{Z-1} |e_k| \right) = 2 SQ^{(i)} SQ^{(1)} \leq \frac{1}{2} d^{i+1} \,,$$

where the first inequality follows from the fact that the two sums on the left-hand side run over every combination of $e_j^{(i)} e_{(k-j) \bmod Z}$, which may have opposite signs, whereas the right-hand side adds the absolute values of all combinations, avoiding any mutual elimination of combinations with opposite signs.

Note that the proof relies on the uniform sequence assumption, i.e., the addresses used to point into the master table have independent uniform distribution. Clearly, this assumption has to be slightly weakened in practice by replacing true randomness with pseudo-randomness. In Theorem 3 we therefore show that we can use pseudo-randomness without compromising security. The idea is to reduce an attack on the Chameleon key stream to an attack on the PRSG itself:

Theorem 3. *Let U be a random variable uniformly distributed over the key symbol space. Let MT be a strongly converging master table. Let the number $s(\lambda')$ of draws from MT be a polynomial function of the security parameter λ' of $\mathcal{CE}$ such that the statistical difference $SQ^{(s)}(\lambda')$ between $X^{(s)}$ and U is a negligible function under the uniform sequence assumption. Then even after replacement of the uniform sequence of addresses with a PRS, no probabilistic polynomial-time adversary can distinguish the pseudo-random key stream consisting of variables $X^{(s)}$ from a truly random key stream with variables U.*

Before we enter into the details of the proof, we clarify the attack goal, the adversary's capabilities, and the criteria for a successful break of (i) a PRSG and (ii) the pseudo-randomness of our Chameleon scheme's key stream:

(i) The goal of an adversary $\mathcal{A}$ attacking a PRSG is to distinguish the output of G on a random seed from a random string of identical length (see Definition 2).

$\mathcal{A}$'s capabilities are limited to a probabilistic Turing machine whose running time is polynomially bounded in the length of its input (and thus also in the security parameter λ, which is defines the input length). A successful break is defined as follows: The challenger $\mathcal{C}$ generates a random seed $str \xleftarrow{R} \{0,1\}^\lambda$ and a random string $str_1 \xleftarrow{R} \{0,1\}^{\mathsf{len}(\lambda)}$ with uniform distribution. $\mathcal{C}$ then applies the PRSG to str and obtains $str_0 \leftarrow \mathsf{G}(str)$. Finally, $\mathcal{C}$ tosses a coin $b \xleftarrow{R} \{0,1\}$ with uniform distribution and sends str_b to $\mathcal{A}$. The challenge for $\mathcal{A}$ is to distinguish the two cases, i.e., guess whether str_b was generated with the PRSG ($b = 0$) or the uniform distribution ($b = 1$). $\mathcal{A}$ wins if the guess b' is equal to b. The advantage of $\mathcal{A}$ is defined as:

$$\mathsf{Adv}(\lambda) := |\mathsf{Pr}[b' = 0|b = 0] - \mathsf{Pr}[b' = 0|b = 1]|, \tag{7}$$

where the randomness is taken over all coin tosses of $\mathcal{C}$ and $\mathcal{A}$.

(ii) The goal of adversary $\mathcal{A}$ attacking the pseudo-randomness of the Chameleon scheme's key stream is to distinguish n instances of $X^{(s)}$ from a truly random key stream. $\mathcal{A}$ is limited to a probabilistic Turing machine whose running time is polynomially bounded in the length of its input (and thus also in the security parameter λ', as this input is given in unary representation). A successful break is defined as follows: The challenger $\mathcal{C}$ generates a stream of n random keys: $K_1 := (k_{1,1}, \ldots, k_{1,n})$ such that $k_{1,j} \xleftarrow{R} \mathcal{K}$ for all $j \in \{1, \ldots, n\}$. Next, $\mathcal{C}$ generates a random seed $str \xleftarrow{R} \{0,1\}^\lambda$ and a strongly converging master table MT. Then $\mathcal{C}$ applies the PRSG to str in order to obtain a pseudo-random sequence of length $\mathsf{len}(\lambda) \geq n \cdot s \cdot l$, which is interpreted as a sequence of $n \cdot s$ addresses in the master table. Subsequently, $\mathcal{C}$ adds for each content coefficient m_j the corresponding s master table entries modulo Z to obtain the other key stream candidate: $K_0 := (k_{0,1}, \ldots, k_{0,n})$ such that $k_{0,j} \leftarrow \sum_{k=1}^{s} mt_{\beta_{j,k}} \bmod Z$. Finally, $\mathcal{C}$ tosses a coin $b \xleftarrow{R} \{0,1\}$ with uniform distribution and sends key stream candidate K_b to $\mathcal{A}$. The challenge for $\mathcal{A}$ is to distinguish the two cases, i.e., guess whether K_b was generated with the Chameleon scheme ($b = 0$) or the uniform distribution ($b = 1$). $\mathcal{A}$ wins if the guess b' is equal to b. The advantage is analogous to (7).

After definition of the attack games, we give the full proof of Theorem 3:

Proof. The proof is by contradiction. Assuming that the advantage of an adversary $\mathcal{A}$ against the pseudo-randomness of the Chameleon scheme's key stream is not negligible, we construct a distinguisher $\mathcal{A}'$ for the PRSG itself, contradicting the assumptions on the PRSG from Definition 2. We show the individual steps of constructing $\mathcal{A}'$ in Fig. 2.

1. The challenger $\mathcal{C}$ generates a random seed $str \xleftarrow{R} \{0,1\}^\lambda$ and a random string $str_1 \xleftarrow{R} \{0,1\}^{\mathsf{len}(\lambda)}$ with uniform distribution. $\mathcal{C}$ then applies the PRSG to str: $str_0 \leftarrow \mathsf{G}(str)$. Finally, $\mathcal{C}$ tosses a coin $b \xleftarrow{R} \{0,1\}$ with uniform distribution.
2. $\mathcal{C}$ sends str_b to $\mathcal{A}'$. $\mathcal{A}'$ needs to guess b.

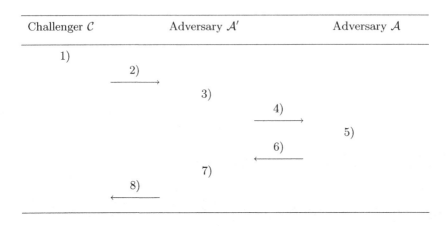

Fig. 2. Construction of adversary $\mathcal{A}'$ based on adversary $\mathcal{A}$

3. $\mathcal{A}'$ generates a strongly converging master table MT. Then $\mathcal{A}'$ takes the string str_b of length $\mathsf{len}(\lambda) \geq n \cdot s \cdot l$ and interprets it as a sequence of $n \cdot s$ addresses in the master table according to (3). Subsequently, $\mathcal{A}'$ adds for each content coefficient m_j the corresponding s master table entries modulo Z to obtain a key stream $K_b := (k_{b,1}, \ldots, k_{b,n})$ such that $k_{b,j} \leftarrow \sum_{k=1}^{s} mt_{\beta_{j,k}} \bmod Z$.
4. $\mathcal{A}'$ sends the key stream K_b to $\mathcal{A}$ as a challenge.
5. $\mathcal{A}$ calculates the guess b', where $b' = 0$ represents the random case, i.e., $\mathcal{A}$ guesses that K_b is a truly random key stream, and $b' = 1$ represents the pseudo-random case, i.e., $\mathcal{A}$ guesses that K_b was generated with the Chameleon scheme.
6. $\mathcal{A}$ sends the guess b' to $\mathcal{A}'$.
7. $\mathcal{A}'$ copies $\mathcal{A}$'s guess.
8. $\mathcal{A}'$ sends b' to $\mathcal{C}$ as a guess for b.

To finish the proof, we need to show that if the advantage of $\mathcal{A}$ against the pseudo-randomness of the Chameleon key stream is not negligible, then the advantage of $\mathcal{A}'$ against the PRSG is not negligible. We prove this by bounding the probability differences in the real attack scenario, where $\mathcal{A}$ is given input by a correct challenger, and the simulated attack, where $\mathcal{A}$ is given slightly incorrect input by $\mathcal{A}'$. The contradictive assumption is that $\mathcal{A}$'s advantage against the Chameleon encryption scheme is not negligible in the real attack:

$$\left| \mathsf{Pr}^{\mathsf{real}}\left[b' = 0 | b = 0\right] - \mathsf{Pr}^{\mathsf{real}}\left[b' = 0 | b = 1\right] \right| \geq \epsilon_{\mathsf{CE}}(\lambda') \,,$$

where $\mathsf{Pr}^{\mathsf{real}}\left[\,\right]$ denotes probabilities in the real attack between a Chameleon challenger and a Chameleon adversary $\mathcal{A}$ and $\epsilon_{\mathsf{CE}}(\lambda')$ is $\mathcal{A}$'s advantage, which is not negligible. The randomness is taken over all coin tosses of $\mathcal{C}$ and $\mathcal{A}$.

Next, we summarize the input to $\mathcal{A}$ in the real attack and the simulated attack. In the real attack, $\mathcal{A}$ obtains either the key stream output K_0 of the Chameleon scheme on a truly random seed str ($b = 0$), or a truly random key stream K_1 ($b = 1$). Specifically, the key stream element $k_{0,j}$ of K_0 is equal to $k_{0,j} = \sum_{k=1}^{s} mt_{\beta_j,k} \mod Z$, where the truly random seed str determines the addresses of the master table entries mt_j via the PRSG according to (3).

In the simulated attack, $\mathcal{A}'$ does not apply the PRSG and instead uses the challenge str_b as a shortcut. $\mathcal{A}$ obtains either the key stream output K_0 of the Chameleon scheme executed on a pseudo-random string str_0, derived from a truly random seed str ($b = 0$), or the key stream output K_1 of the Chameleon scheme executed on a truly random string str_1 ($b = 1$). The key stream outputs K_0 and K_1 in the simulated attack thus only differ by the fact that K_0 comes from a pseudo-random string and K_1 from a truly random string.

There is no difference between real and simulated attack for $b = 0$. The key stream outputs K_0^{real} and K_0^{sim} both come from a PRSG executed on a truly random seed str, leading to the following relation:

$$\left| \mathsf{Pr}^{\text{real}} \left[b' = 0 | b = 0 \right] - \mathsf{Pr}^{\text{sim}} \left[b' = 0 | b = 0 \right] \right| = 0 ,$$

where the randomness is taken over all coin tosses of $\mathcal{C}$ and $\mathcal{A}$ in the real attack and those of $\mathcal{C}$, $\mathcal{A}'$ and $\mathcal{A}$ in the simulated attack.

For $b = 1$ and a real attack, $\mathcal{A}$ obtains a truly random key stream K_1^{real}. In the simulated attack, $\mathcal{A}'$ operates on a truly random string str_1 that determines $n \cdot s$ addresses according to (3). As str_1 is truly random, the $n \cdot s$ addresses are also truly random with independent uniform distribution. Combined with the assumptions of the theorem, this implies that each pair of key stream elements in real and simulated attack has a negligible statistical difference. Negligible statistical difference implies polynomial-time indistinguishability [24, Section 3.2.2]. Let $\epsilon_{\text{diff}}(\lambda')$ be the corresponding negligible bound on the advantage of a distinguisher, which applies for one key stream element. Then the difference between both attacks for all n key stream elements has a negligible upper bound $n \cdot \epsilon_{\text{diff}}(\lambda')$:

$$\left| \mathsf{Pr}^{\text{real}} \left[b' = 0 | b = 1 \right] - \mathsf{Pr}^{\text{sim}} \left[b' = 0 | b = 1 \right] \right| \le n \cdot \epsilon_{\text{diff}}(\lambda') ,$$

where the randomness is taken over all coin tosses of $\mathcal{C}$ and $\mathcal{A}$ in the real attack and those of $\mathcal{C}$, $\mathcal{A}'$ and $\mathcal{A}$ in the simulated attack.

The last three inequalities lead to a lower bound for the success probability of $\mathcal{A}$ in the simulated attack, which is also the success probability of $\mathcal{A}'$ in the attack against the PRSG:

$$\left| \mathsf{Pr}^{\text{sim}} \left[b' = 0 | b = 0 \right] - \mathsf{Pr}^{\text{sim}} \left[b' = 0 | b = 1 \right] \right| \ge \epsilon_{\text{CE}}(\lambda') - n \cdot \epsilon_{\text{diff}}(\lambda')$$

As $\epsilon_{\text{CE}}(\lambda')$ is not negligible by the contradictive assumption, $\epsilon_{\text{diff}}(\lambda')$ is negligible by the negligible statistical difference and n is a constant, we conclude that the success probability of $\mathcal{A}'$ against the PRSG is not negligible, completing the contradiction and the proof.

5   Implementation

The master table MT obviously becomes strongly converging for sufficiently large L. Our simulation shows that $L = 4Z$ gives high assurance of strong convergence. However, lower values still lead to weak convergence in the sense that it is not proven by our upper bound, but can easily be verified numerically. As discussed in Section 4.2 we need to choose the number s of draws from MT in accordance with L. The upper bound in Theorem 6 is too conservative to choose s in practice. Our simulation shows that the statistical difference $SQ^{(s)}$ not only decreases with factor $d \approx 2SQ^{(1)} < 1$, but with an even smaller factor. This is due to the fact that some of the combinations $e_j^{(i)} e_{(k-j) \bmod Z}$ on the left-hand side of the inequality in the proof of Lemma 6 cancel out. In Appendix F we therefore give an explicit formula for calculation of the *exact* statistical difference after s draws from MT. The center can thus generate MT with arbitrary length L, numerically verify convergence and determine the minimum number of draws s_{min} that provides the desired statistical difference.

The content representation can be extended to cover movies and songs by interpreting them as a sequence of content items. A straightforward approach is to regularly refresh the session key. While further refinements are possible, aiming to prevent sequence-specific attacks such as averaging across movie frames, they are beyond the scope of this document. However, it remains to define how the insignificant part of the content should be processed (see Section 3.2). There are three obvious options: sending it in the clear, passing it through our scheme or encrypting it separately. Note that by its very definition, this part does not give significant information about the content and was not watermarked because the coefficients do not have perceptible influence on the reassembled content. The easiest option is thus to pass them through the proposed scheme, which does not influence goodness and maintains confidentiality of the content.

At first sight our proposed scheme trivially fulfills the correctness requirement (see Definition 4) due to the correctness of the SSW scheme. However, both schemes face difficulties in the rare event that a content coefficient is at the lower or upper end of the interval $[0, z]$, which corresponds with plaintext symbols close to 0 or $Z - 1$. If the additive fingerprint coefficient causes a trespass of lower or upper bound, the SSW scheme needs to decrease the coefficient's amplitude and round to the corresponding bound. Similarly, our scheme must avoid a wrap-around in the additive group, e.g., when plaintext symbol $Z - 2$ obtains a coefficient of $+3$ and ends up at 1 after decryption. There are many options with different security trade-offs, such as sending a flag or even sending the coefficient in cleartext; the appropriate choice depends on further requirements of the implementation. Note that the center trivially anticipates the occurrence of a wrap-around from inspecting the content coefficients.

5.1 Efficiency

Three performance parameters determine whether the proposed scheme is efficient and implementable: transmission overhead, storage size of a receiver, and computation cost. We stress that our scheme enables a tradeoff between storage size and computation cost. Increasing the size L of the master table (and thus the storage size) decreases the necessary number s of draws (and thus the computation cost), as can be seen from Lemma 6 and Definition 8, where $SQ^{(1)}$ and thus d decreases with L. This feature allows us to adapt the scheme to the particular constraints of the receiver, in particular to decrease s.

The transmission overhead of the Chameleon scheme is 0 if the master table and receiver tables are not renewed on a regular basis. In this scenario, the Chameleon scheme's transmission overhead is 0 because ciphertext and cleartext use the same symbol space and thus have the same length; the transmission overhead of fingercasting is thus determined by that of the broadcast encryption scheme, which is moderate [5,6,7,8].[8]

For the storage size, we highlight the parameters of a computation-intensive implementation. Let the content be an image with $n = 10,000$ significant coefficients of 16 bit length, such that $Z = 2^{16}$. By testing several lengths L of the master table MT, we found a statistical quality of $SQ^{(1)} = d/2 < 1/8$ for $L = 8 \cdot Z = 8 \cdot 2^{16} = 2^{19} = 2^l$. A receiver table thus has $2^{19} \cdot 16 = 2^{23}$ bit or 2^{20} Byte $= 2^{10}$ kByte $= 1$ MByte, which seems acceptable in practice.

The computation cost depends mostly on the number s of draws from the master table. To achieve a small statistical difference $SQ^{(s)}$, e.g., below 2^{-128}, we choose $s = 64$ and therefore $SQ^{(s)} < 1/2 \cdot d^s = 2^{-1} \cdot 2^{-2 \cdot 64} = 2^{-129}$ by the conservative upper bound of Lemma 6. Compared to a conventional stream cipher that encrypts $n \cdot \log_2 Z$ bits, a receiver has to generate $n \cdot s \cdot l$ pseudo-random bits, which is an overhead of $(s \cdot l)/\log_2 Z = 76$. To generate the pseudo-random key stream, the receiver has to perform $n \cdot s$ table lookups and $n \cdot (s+1)$ modular operations in a group of size 2^{16}.

In further tests, we also found a more storage-intensive implementation with $L = 2^{25}$ and $s = 25$, which leads to 64 MBytes of storage and an overhead of $(s \cdot l)/\log_2 Z \approx 39$. By calculating the exact statistical difference of Appendix F instead of the conservative upper bound of Lemma 6, s decreases further, but we are currently unaware of any direct formula to calculate s based on a master table length L and a desired statistical difference $SQ^{(s)}$ (or vice versa).

If the security requirements of an implementation require a regular renewal of the master table and the subsequent redistribution of the receiver tables, then the transmission overhead obviously increases. For each redistribution, the total key material to be transmitted has the size of the master table times the number of receivers. As mentioned before, a redistribution channel then becomes necessary if the broadcast channel does not have enough spare bandwidth.

---

[8] For example, this overhead is far smaller than that of the trivial solution, which consists of sequentially sending an individually fingerprinted copy of the content individually encrypted over the broadcast channel.

6   Conclusion and Open Problems

In this document we gave a formal proof of the security of a new Chameleon cipher. Applied to a generic fingercasting approach, it provides confidentiality of ciphertext, traceability of content and keys as well as renewability. We achieved confidentiality through a combination of a generic broadcast encryption (BE) scheme and the new Chameleon cipher. The BE scheme provides a fresh session key, which the Chameleon scheme uses to generate a pseudo-random key stream. The pseudo-random key stream arises from adding key symbols at pseudo-random addresses in a long master table, initially filled with random key symbols. We have reduced the security of the pseudo-random key stream to that of a pseudo-random sequence generator.

In addition, we achieved traceability of keys and content through embedding of a receiver-specific fingerprint into the master table copies, which are given to the receivers. During decryption, these fingerprints are inevitably embedded into the content, enabling the tracing of malicious users. We achieve the same collusion resistance as an exemplary watermarking scheme with proven security bound. It may be replaced with any fingerprinting scheme whose watermarks can be decomposed into additive components. Finally, we achieved renewability through revocation, which is performed in the BE scheme.

Two open problems are the most promising for future work. First of all, the detection algorithm should be extended in order to allow blind detection of a watermark even in the absence of the original content. Another open problem is to combine Chameleon encryption with a code-based fingerprinting scheme in the sense of Boneh and Shaw [29]. The master table in Chameleon would need to embed components of codewords in such a way that a codeword is embedded into the content.

References

1. Adelsbach, A., Huber, U., Sadeghi, A.R.: Fingercasting—joint fingerprinting and decryption of broadcast messages. Tenth Australasian Conference on Information Security and Privacy—ACISP 2006, Melbourne, Australia, July 3-5, 2006. Volume 4058 of Lecture Notes in Computer Science, Springer (2006)
2. Touretzky, D.S.: Gallery of CSS descramblers. Webpage, Computer Science Department of Carnegie Mellon University (2000) URL http://www.cs.cmu.edu/~dst/DeCSS/Gallery (November 17, 2005).
3. 4C Entity, LLC: CPPM specification—introduction and common cryptographic elements. Specification Revision 1.0 (2003) URL http://www.4centity.com/data/tech/spec/cppm-base100.pdf.
4. AACS Licensing Administrator: Advanced access content system (AACS): Introduction and common cryptographic elements. Specification Revision 0.90 (2005) URL http://www.aacsla.com/specifications/AACS_Spec-Common_0.90.pdf.
5. Fiat, A., Naor, M.: Broadcast encryption. In Stinson, D.R., ed.: CRYPTO 1993. Volume 773 of Lecture Notes in Computer Science, Springer (1994) 480–491
6. Naor, D., Naor, M., Lotspiech, J.: Revocation and tracing schemes for stateless receivers. In Kilian, J., ed.: CRYPTO 2001. Volume 2139 of Lecture Notes in Computer Science, Springer (2001) 41–62

7. Halevy, D., Shamir, A.: The LSD broadcast encryption scheme. In Yung, M., ed.: CRYPTO 2002. Volume 2442 of Lecture Notes in Computer Science, Springer (2002) 47–60

8. Jho, N.S., Hwang, J.Y., Cheon, J.H., Kim, M.H., Lee, D.H., Yoo, E.S.: One-way chain based broadcast encryption schemes. In Cramer, R., ed.: EUROCRYPT 2005. Volume 3494 of Lecture Notes in Computer Science, Springer (2005) 559–574

9. Chor, B., Fiat, A., Naor, M.: Tracing traitors. In Desmedt, Y., ed.: CRYPTO 1994. Volume 839 of Lecture Notes in Computer Science, Springer (1994) 257–270

10. Naor, M., Pinkas, B.: Threshold traitor tracing. In Krawczyk, H., ed.: CRYPTO 1998. Volume 1462 of Lecture Notes in Computer Science, Springer (1998) 502–517

11. Kundur, D., Karthik, K.: Video fingerprinting and encryption principles for digital rights management. Proceedings of the IEEE **92**(6) (2004) 918–932

12. Anderson, R.J., Manifavas, C.: Chameleon—a new kind of stream cipher. In Biham, E., ed.: FSE 1997. Volume 1267 of Lecture Notes in Computer Science, Springer (1997) 107–113

13. Briscoe, B., Fairman, I.: Nark: Receiver-based multicast non-repudiation and key management. In: ACM EC 1999, ACM Press (1999) 22–30

14. Cox, I.J., Kilian, J., Leighton, T., Shamoon, T.: Secure spread spectrum watermarking for multimedia. IEEE Transactions on Image Processing **6**(12) (1997) 1673–1687

15. Kilian, J., Leighton, F.T., Matheson, L.R., Shamoon, T.G., Tarjan, R.E., Zane, F.: Resistance of digital watermarks to collusive attacks. Technical Report TR-585-98, Princeton University, Department of Computer Science (1998) URL: ftp://ftp.cs.princeton.edu/techreports/1998/585.ps.gz.

16. Anderson, R.J., Kuhn, M.: Tamper resistance—a cautionary note. In Tygar, D., ed.: USENIX Electronic Commerce 1996, USENIX (1996) 1–11

17. Maurer, U.M.: A provably-secure strongly-randomized cipher. In Damgård, I., ed.: EUROCRYPT 1990. Volume 473 of Lecture Notes in Computer Science, Springer (1990) 361–373

18. Maurer, U.: Conditionally-perfect secrecy and a provably-secure randomized cipher. Journal of Cryptology **5**(1) (1992) 53–66

19. Ferguson, N., Schneier, B., Wagner, D.: Security weaknesses in a randomized stream cipher. In Dawson, E., Clark, A., Boyd, C., eds.: ACISP 2000. Volume 1841 of Lecture Notes in Computer Science, Springer (2000) 234–241

20. Ergün, F., Kilian, J., Kumar, R.: A note on the limits of collusion-resistant watermarks. In Stern, J., ed.: EUROCRYPT 1999. Volume 1592 of Lecture Notes in Computer Science, Springer (1999) 140–149

21. Brown, I., Perkins, C., Crowcroft, J.: Watercasting: Distributed watermarking of multicast media. In Rizzo, L., Fdida, S., eds.: Networked Group Communication 1999. Volume 1736 of Lecture Notes in Computer Science, Springer (1999) 286–300

22. Parviainen, R., Parnes, P.: Large scale distributed watermarking of multicast media through encryption. In Steinmetz, R., Dittmann, J., Steinebach, M., eds.: Communications and Multimedia Security (CMS 2001). Volume 192 of IFIP Conference Proceedings., International Federation for Information Processing, Communications and Multimedia Security (IFIP), Kluwer (2001) 149–158

23. Luh, W., Kundur, D.: New paradigms for effective multicasting and fingerprinting of entertainment media. IEEE Communications Magazine **43**(5) (2005) 77–84

24. Goldreich, O.: Basic Tools. First edn. Volume 1 of Foundations of Cryptography. Cambridge University Press, Cambridge, UK (2001)

25. Bellare, M., Namprempre, C.: Authenticated encryption: Relations among notions and analysis of the generic composition paradigm. In Okamoto, T., ed.: ASIACRYPT 2000. Volume 1976 of Lecture Notes in Computer Science, Springer (2000) 531–545
26. National Institute of Standards and Technology, *Announcing the Advanced Encryption Standard (AES)*, Federal Information Processing Standards Publication FIPS PUB 197, November 26, 2001, URL http://csrc.nist.gov/publications/fips/fips197/fips-197.pdf .
27. National Institute of Standards and Technology, *Data Encryption Standard (DES)*, Federal Information Processing Standards Publication FIPS PUB 46-3, October 25, 1999, URL http://csrc.nist.gov/publications/fips/fips46-3/fips46-3.pdf .
28. Goldreich, O.: Basic Applications. First edn. Volume 2 of Foundations of Cryptography. Cambridge University Press, Cambridge, UK (2004)
29. Boneh, D., Shaw, J.: Collusion-secure fingerprinting for digital data (extended abstract). In Coppersmith, D., ed.: CRYPTO 1995. Volume 963 of Lecture Notes in Computer Science, Springer (1995) 452–465

A   Abbreviations

Table 1 summarizes all abbreviations used in this document.

Table 1. Abbreviations used in this document

Abbreviation	Abbreviated Technical Term
AACS	Advanced Access Content System
AES	Advanced Encryption Standard
BE	Broadcast Encryption
CPPM	Content Protection for Pre-Recorded Media
CRL	Certificate Revocation List
CSS	Content Scrambling System
DCT	Discrete Cosine Transform
DES	Data Encryption Standard
DVD	Digital Versatile Disc
FE	Fingerprint Embedding
PRS	Pseudo-Random Sequence
PRSG	Pseudo-Random Sequence Generator
SSW	Spread Spectrum Watermarking
TV	Television

B   Summary of Relevant Parameters

Table 2 summarizes all parameters of our fingercasting approach and the underlying fingerprinting scheme, which we instantiate with the SSW scheme of [15].

Table 2. Parameters of the proposed fingercasting scheme and the SSW scheme

Parameter	Description
N	Number of receivers
u_i	i-th receiver
q	Maximum tolerable number of colluding receivers
M	Representation of the original content
m_j	j-th coefficient of content M
n	Number of coefficients (Chameleon scheme)
n'	Number of coefficients (fingerprinting scheme)
$CF^{(i)}$	Content fingerprint of receiver u_i
$cf_j^{(i)}$	Coefficient j of u_i's content fingerprint $CF^{(i)}$
M^*	Illegal copy of the original content
CF^*	Fingerprint found in an illegal copy M^*
C	Ciphertext of the original content M
c_j	j-th coefficient of ciphertext C
k^{sess}	Session key used as a seed for the PRSG
MT	Master table of the Chameleon scheme
α	Address of a table entry
mt_α	α-th entry of the master table MT
$TF^{(i)}$	Table fingerprint for receiver table of receiver u_i
$tf_\alpha^{(i)}$	h-th coefficient of u_i's table fingerprint $TF^{(i)}$
$RT^{(i)}$	Receiver table of receiver u_i
$rt_\alpha^{(i)}$	α-th entry of the receiver table $RT^{(i)}$
l	Number of bits needed for the binary address of a table entry
L	Number of entries of the tables, $L = 2^l$
F	Number of fingerprinted entries of a receiver table
s	Number of master table entries per ciphertext coefficient
par_{CE}	Input parameters (Chameleon scheme)
par_{FP}	Input parameters (fingerprinting scheme)
σ	Standard deviation for receiver table
σ'	Standard deviation for SSW scheme
p^{bad}	Maximum probability of a bad copy
p^{pos}	Maximum probability of a false positive
p^{neg}	Maximum probability of a false negative
δ	Goodness criterion (SSW scheme)
t	Threshold of similarity measure (SSW scheme)
dec	Decision output of detection algorithm
z	Upper bound of interval $[0, z]$ (content coefficients)
Z	Key space size and cardinality of discrete interval $[0, z]$
ρ	Scaling factor from real numbers to group elements
p	Order of the additive group

C　Chameleon Encryption

Definition 9. *A* Chameleon encryption scheme *is a tuple of five polynomial-time algorithms* $\mathcal{CE} := (\mathsf{KeyGenCE}, \mathsf{KeyExtrCE}, \mathsf{EncCE}, \mathsf{DecCE}, \mathsf{DetectCE})$, *where:*

- $\mathsf{KeyGenCE}$ *is the* probabilistic *key generation algorithm used by the center to set up all parameters of the scheme.* $\mathsf{KeyGenCE}$ *takes the number N of receivers, a security parameter λ', and a set of performance parameters par_{CE} as input in order to generate a secret master table MT, a tuple $TF := (TF^{(1)}, \ldots, TF^{(N)})$ of secret table fingerprints containing one fingerprint per receiver, and a threshold t. The values N and λ' are public:*

$$(MT, TF, t) \leftarrow \mathsf{KeyGenCE}(N, 1^{\lambda'}, par_{\mathsf{CE}})$$

- $\mathsf{KeyExtrCE}$ *is the* deterministic *key extraction algorithm used by the center to extract the secret receiver table $RT^{(i)}$ to be delivered to receiver u_i in the setup phase.* $\mathsf{KeyExtrCE}$ *takes the master table MT, the table fingerprints TF, and the index i of receiver u_i as input in order to return $RT^{(i)}$:*

$$RT^{(i)} \leftarrow \mathsf{KeyExtrCE}(MT, TF, i)$$

- EncCE *is the* deterministic *encryption algorithm used by the center to encrypt content M such that only receivers in possession of a receiver table and the session key can recover it.* EncCE *takes the master table MT, a session key k^{sess}, and content M as input in order to return the ciphertext C:*

$$C \leftarrow \mathsf{EncCE}(MT, k^{\mathsf{sess}}, M)$$

- DecCE *is the* deterministic *decryption algorithm used by a receiver u_i to decrypt a ciphertext C.* DecCE *takes the receiver table $RT^{(i)}$ of receiver u_i, a session key k^{sess}, and a ciphertext C as input. It returns a good copy $M^{(i)}$ of the underlying content M if C is a valid encryption of M using k^{sess}:*

$$M^{(i)} \leftarrow \mathsf{DecCE}(RT^{(i)}, k^{\mathsf{sess}}, C)$$

- $\mathsf{DetectCE}$ *is the* deterministic *fingerprint detection algorithm used by the center to detect whether the table fingerprint $TF^{(i)}$ of receiver u_i left traces in an illegal copy M^*.* $\mathsf{DetectCE}$ *takes the original content M, the illegal copy M^*, the session key k^{sess}, the table fingerprint $TF^{(i)}$ of u_i, and the threshold t as input in order to return $dec = \mathtt{true}$ if the similarity measure of the underlying fingerprinting scheme indicates that the similarity between M^* and $M^{(i)}$ is above the threshold t. Otherwise it returns $dec = \mathtt{false}$:*

$$dec \leftarrow \mathsf{DetectCE}(M, M^*, k^{\mathsf{sess}}, TF^{(i)}, t)$$

Correctness of $\mathcal{CE}$ requires that

$$\forall u_i \in \mathcal{U}: \ \mathsf{DecCE}(RT^{(i)}, k^{\mathsf{sess}}, \mathsf{EncCE}(MT, k^{\mathsf{sess}}, M)) = M^{(i)} \quad \text{such that}$$
$$\mathsf{Good}(M^{(i)}, M) = \mathtt{true} \quad \text{(see Definition 3) with high probability.}$$

D   Fingerprinting and Spread Spectrum Watermarking

In this section, we detail our notation of a fingerprinting scheme by describing the respective algorithms of Spread Spectrum Watermarking [14,15]. This scheme is a tuple of three polynomial-time algorithms (SetupFP, EmbedFP, DetectFP). We detail each of the three algorithms in Sections D.1–D.3.

D.1   Setup Algorithm

SetupFP is the probabilistic setup algorithm used by the center to set up all parameters of the scheme. SetupFP takes the number N of receivers, the number n' of content coefficients, a goodness criterion δ, a maximum probability p^{bad} of bad copies, and a maximum probability p^{pos} of false positives as input in order to return a tuple of secret content fingerprints CF, containing one fingerprint per receiver, as well as a similarity threshold t. The values N and n' are public:

$$(CF, t) \leftarrow \mathsf{SetupFP}(N, n', \delta, p^{\mathsf{bad}}, p^{\mathsf{pos}})$$

The algorithm of [14,15] proceeds as follows. The set of content fingerprints CF is defined as $CF := (CF^{(1)}, \ldots, CF^{(N)})$. The content fingerprint $CF^{(i)}$ of receiver u_i is a vector $CF^{(i)} := (cf_1^{(i)}, \ldots, cf_{n'}^{(i)})$ of n' fingerprint coefficients. For each receiver index $i \in \{1, \ldots, N\}$ and for each coefficient index $j \in \{1, \ldots, n'\}$, the fingerprint coefficient follows an independent normal distribution. The standard deviation of this distribution depends on the values N, n', δ, and p^{bad}:

$$\forall 1 \leq i \leq N, \forall 1 \leq j \leq n' : \quad cf_j^{(i)} \leftarrow \mathsf{N}(0, \sigma') \quad \text{with} \quad \sigma' = \mathsf{f}_{\sigma'}(N, n', \delta, p^{\mathsf{bad}})$$

The similarity threshold t is a function $t = \mathsf{f}_t(\sigma', N, p^{\mathsf{pos}})$ of σ', N, and p^{pos}. The details of $\mathsf{f}_{\sigma'}$ and f_t can be found in [15].

D.2   Watermark Embedding Algorithm

EmbedFP is the deterministic watermark embedding algorithm used by the center to embed the content fingerprint $CF^{(i)}$ of receiver u_i into the original content M. EmbedFP takes the original content M and the secret content fingerprint $CF^{(i)}$ of receiver u_i as input in order to return the fingerprinted copy $M^{(i)}$ of u_i:

$$M^{(i)} \leftarrow \mathsf{EmbedFP}(M, CF^{(i)})$$

The algorithm of [14,15] adds the fingerprint coefficient to the original content coefficient to obtain the fingerprinted content coefficient:

$$\forall j \in \{1, \ldots, n'\} : \quad m_j^{(i)} \leftarrow m_j + cf_j^{(i)}$$

D.3   Watermark Detection Algorithm

DetectFP is the deterministic watermark detection algorithm used by the center to verify whether an illegal content copy M^* contains traces of the content fingerprint $CF^{(i)}$ that was embedded into the content copy $M^{(i)}$ of receiver u_i. DetectFP takes the original content M, the illegal copy M^*, the content fingerprint $CF^{(i)}$, and the similarity threshold t as input and returns the decision $dec \in \{\texttt{true}, \texttt{false}\}$:

$$dec \leftarrow \mathsf{DetectFP}(M, M^*, CF^{(i)}, t)$$

The algorithm of [14,15] calculates the similarity measure between the fingerprint in the illegal copy and the fingerprint of the suspect receiver. The similarity measure is defined as the dot product between the two fingerprints, divided by the Euclidean norm of the fingerprint in the illegal copy:

$$CF^* \leftarrow M^* - M$$
$$\mathsf{Sim}(CF^*, CF^{(i)}) \leftarrow \frac{CF^* \cdot CF^{(i)}}{\|CF^*\|}$$

If $\mathsf{Sim}(CF^*, CF^{(i)}) > t$

Then Return $dec = \texttt{true}$

Else Return $dec = \texttt{false}$

E   Broadcast Encryption

In this section we describe a general BE scheme that allows revocation of an arbitrary subset of the set of receivers. Examples for such BE schemes are [6,7,8]. As these schemes all belong to the family of subset cover schemes defined in [6], we use this name to refer to them:

Definition 10. *A* Subset Cover BE (SCBE) *scheme is a tuple of four polynomial-time algorithms (*KeyGenBE, KeyExtrBE, EncBE, DecBE*), where:*

- KeyGenBE *is the probabilistic* key generation *algorithm used by the center to set up all parameters of the scheme.* KeyGenBE *takes the number N of receivers and a security parameter λ'' as input in order to generate the secret master key MK. The values N and λ'' are public:*

$$MK \leftarrow \mathsf{KeyGenBE}(N, 1^{\lambda''})$$

- KeyExtrBE *is the deterministic* key extraction *algorithm used by the center to extract the secret key $SK^{(i)}$ to be delivered to a receiver u_i in the setup phase.* KeyExtrBE *takes the master key MK and the receiver index i as input in order to return the secret key $SK^{(i)}$ of u_i:*

$$SK^{(i)} \leftarrow \mathsf{KeyExtrBE}(MK, i)$$

- EncBE *is the deterministic* encryption *algorithm used to encrypt session key k^{sess} in such a way that only the non-revoked receivers can recover it.* EncBE *takes the master key MK, the set $\mathcal{R}$ of revoked receivers, and session key k^{sess} as input in order to return the ciphertext C_{BE}:*

$$C_{\mathsf{BE}} \leftarrow \mathsf{EncBE}(MK, \mathcal{R}, k^{\mathsf{sess}})$$

– DecBE *is the deterministic decryption algorithm used by a receiver u_i to decrypt a ciphertext C_{BE}.* DecBE *takes the index i of u_i, its private key $SK^{(i)}$, and a ciphertext C_{BE} as input in order to return the session key k^{sess} if C_{BE} is a valid encryption of k^{sess} and u_i is non-revoked, i.e., $u_i \notin \mathcal{R}$. Otherwise, it returns the failure symbol $\bot$:*

$$k^{sess} \leftarrow \mathsf{DecBE}(i, SK^{(i)}, C_{BE}) \quad if \quad u_i \notin \mathcal{R}$$

Correctness of a SCBE scheme requires that

$$\forall u_i \in \mathcal{U} \setminus \mathcal{R}: \quad \mathsf{DecBE}(i, SK^{(i)}, \mathsf{EncBE}(MK, \mathcal{R}, k^{sess})) = k^{sess}.$$

F   Selection of the Minimum Number of Draws

The center can calculate the statistical difference after s draws if it knows the corresponding probability distribution. The next lemma gives an explicit formula for this probability distribution. To determine the minimum number of draws to achieve a maximum statistical difference, e.g., 2^{-128}, the center increases s until the statistical difference is below the desired maximum. Note that this only needs to be done once at setup time of the system when s is chosen.

Lemma 7. *If the draws use addresses with independent uniform distribution and the master table MT is given in the representation of Lemma 5, then the drawing and adding of s master table entries leads to the random variable*

$$X^{(s)} := \left(\sum_{j=1}^{s} X_j \right) \bmod Z \quad with$$

$$\Pr\left[X^{(s)} = x \right] = \sum_{\text{condition}} \binom{s}{s_0, \dots, s_{Z-1}} \prod_{k=0}^{Z-1} p_k{}^{s_k}$$

where condition $\Leftrightarrow$ (8) $\wedge$ (9) $\wedge$ (10) :

$$s_k \geq 0 \quad \forall k \in \{0, 1, \dots, Z-1\} \tag{8}$$

$$\sum_{k=0}^{Z-1} s_k = s \tag{9}$$

$$\left(\sum_{k=0}^{Z-1} s_k \cdot x_k \right) \bmod Z = x, \tag{10}$$

where s_k denotes the number of times that key space element x_k was chosen in the s selections and $\binom{s}{s_0, \dots, s_{Z-1}} := \frac{s!}{s_0! \cdot \dots \cdot s_{Z-1}!}$ denotes the multinomial coefficient.

Proof. Each of the s selections is a random variable X_j with $\Pr[X_j = x_k] = p_k$. The independence of the random addresses transfers to the independence of the X_j. The probability of a complete set of s selections is thus a product of s probabilities of the form $\prod_1^s p$ with appropriate indices. The counter s_k stores the number of times that probability p_k appears in this term. This counter is non-negative, implying(8). In total, there are s selections, implying (9).

To fulfill the condition $X^{(s)} = x$, the addition modulo Z of the s random variables must have the result x. Given the counters s_k, the result of the addition is $(\sum_{k=0}^{Z-1} s_k \cdot x_k) \bmod Z$. The combination of both statements implies (10).

There is more than one possibility for selecting s_k times the key symbol x_k during the s selections. Considering all such key symbols in s selections, the total number of possibilities is the number of ways in which we can choose s_0 times the key symbol x_0, then s_1 times the key symbol x_1, and so forth until we reach a total of s selections. This number is the multinomial coefficient $\binom{s}{s_0,\ldots,s_{Z-1}}$.

Note that we can trivially verify that the probabilities of all key space elements x in Lemma 7 add to 1. Among the three conditions (8), (9), and (10), the first two conditions appear in the well-known multinomial theorem

$$(\sum_{k=0}^{Z-1} p_k)^s = \sum_{\substack{s_0,\ldots,s_{Z-1} \geq 0 \\ s_0+\ldots+s_{Z-1}=s}} \binom{s}{s_0,\ldots,s_{Z-1}} \prod_{k=0}^{Z-1} p_k^{s_k}$$

By adding the probabilities over all elements, we obviously add over all addends on the right-hand side of the multinomial theorem. As the left-hand side trivially adds to 1, so do the probabilities over all key space elements.

An Estimation Attack on Content-Based Video Fingerprinting

Shan He[1] and Darko Kirovski[2]

[1] Department of Electrical and Computer Engineering
University of Maryland, College Park, MD 20742 U.S.A
[2] Microsoft Research, One Microsoft Way, Redmond WA 98052 U.S.A
shanhe@eng.umd.edu, darkok@microsoft.com

Abstract. In this paper we propose a simple signal processing procedure that aims at removing low-frequency fingerprints embedded in video signals. Although we construct an instance of the attack and show its efficacy using a specific video fingerprinting algorithm, the generic form of the attack can be applied to an arbitrary video marking scheme. The proposed attack uses two estimates: one of the embedded fingerprint and another of the original content, to create the attack vector. This vector is amplified and subtracted from the fingerprinted video sequence to create the attacked copy. The amplification factor is maximized under the constraint of achieving a desired level of visual fidelity. In the conducted experiments, the attack procedure on the average halved the expected detector correlation compared to additive white gaussian noise. It also substantially increased the probability of a false positive under attack for the addressed fingerprinting algorithm.

Keywords: Video watermarking, fingerprinting, signal estimation.

1 Introduction

Content watermarking is a signal processing primitive where a secret noise signal $\mathbf{w}$ is added to the original multimedia sequence $\mathbf{x}$ so that: (*i*) perceptually, the watermarked content $\mathbf{y} = \mathbf{x} + \mathbf{w}$ is indistinguishable from the original and (*ii*) watermark detection produces low error rates both in terms of false positives and negatives. An additional requirement is that the watermark should be detected reliably in marked content even after an arbitrary signal processing primitive $f()$ is applied to $\mathbf{y}$ such that $f(\mathbf{y})$ is a perceptually acceptable copy of $\mathbf{x}$. Function $f()$ is constructed without the knowledge of $\mathbf{w}$.

Content fingerprinting is a specific application of content watermarking with an objective to produce many unique content copies. Each copy is associated with a particular system user. Thus, a discovered content copy that is illegally used, can be traced to its associated user. Here, a distinct watermark $\mathbf{w}_i$ (i.e., a fingerprint) is applied to $\mathbf{x}$ to create a unique content copy $\mathbf{y}_i$. We will denote the set of all fingerprints as $\mathbb{W} = \{\mathbf{w}_1, \ldots, \mathbf{w}_M\}$ published in $\mathbb{Y} = \{\mathbf{y}_1, \ldots, \mathbf{y}_M\}$. The fingerprint detector $d(\mathbf{x}, f(\mathbf{y}_i), \mathbb{W})$ should return the index of the user i associated with the content under

Y.Q. Shi (Eds.): Transactions on DHMS II, LNCS 4499, pp. 35–47, 2007.

test $\mathbf{y}_i$. Typically, this decision is associated with a confidence level which must be high. In particular, one demands low probability of false positives:

$$\Pr[d(\mathbf{x}, f(\mathbf{y}_i), \mathbb{W}) = j, j \neq i] < \varepsilon_{FP}, \qquad (1)$$

where ε_{FP} is typically smaller than 10^{-9}. In case a content copy $\hat{\mathbf{y}}$ which is not marked with any of the fingerprints in $\mathbb{W}$, is fed to the detector, it should report that no fingerprint is identified in $\hat{\mathbf{y}}$: $d(\mathbf{x}, \hat{\mathbf{y}}, \mathbb{W}) = 0$ with high confidence. Finally, the detector uses the knowledge of the original $\mathbf{x}$ while making its decision. This feature substantially improves the accuracy of the forensic detector compared to "blind" detectors [1] which are prone to de-synchronization attacks [2].

Attacks against fingerprinting technologies can be divided into two classes: collusion and fingerprint removal. A collusion attack considers an adversarial clique $\mathbb{Q} \subset \mathbb{Y}$ of a certain size K. The participating colluders compare their fingerprinted copies to produce a new attack copy which does not include statistically important traces of any of their fingerprints [3, 4]. Another objective that a collusion clique may have, is to frame an innocent colluder. Collusion attacks have attracted great deal of attention from the research community which has mainly focused on producing codes that result in improved collusion resistance [5, 6, 7, 8, 9].

1.1 Fingerprint Estimation

In this paper we address the other class of attacks on multimedia forensic schemes: *fingerprint removal via estimation*. Here, the adversary has the objective to estimate the value of a given fingerprint $\mathbf{w}_i$ based upon $\mathbf{y}_i$ only and without the presence of $d()$. In essence, this attack aims at denoising $\mathbf{y}_i$ from its fingerprint. In order to make denoising attacks harder, one may design fingerprints dependent upon $\mathbf{x}$ so that it is more difficult to estimate them accurately. The effects of this class of attacks are orthogonal to collusion. An adversarial clique may deploy both types of attacks to achieve its goal: Estimation, to reduce the presence of individual fingerprints in their respective copies, and collusion, to perform the removal of the remaining fingerprint traces by creating a final attack copy.

For example, a forensic application that uses spread-spectrum fingerprints $\mathbf{w}_i \in \{\pm 1\}^N$, where N is sequence length, detects them using a correlation based detector $c(\mathbf{x}, \mathbf{a}, \mathbf{w}_i) = N^{-1}(\mathbf{a} - \mathbf{x}) \cdot \mathbf{w}_i$, where $\mathbf{a}$ is the content under test and operator '·' denotes an inner product of two vectors [1]. Content $\mathbf{a}$ is a result of forensic multimedia registration exemplified in [4]. In case $\mathbf{a}$ is marked with $\mathbf{w}_i$, we model $\mathbf{a} = \mathbf{x} + \mathbf{w}_i + \mathbf{n}$, where $\mathbf{n}$ is a low magnitude gaussian noise. Under the assumption that $\mathrm{E}[\mathbf{n} \cdot \mathbf{w}_i] = 0$, we have $\mathrm{E}[c(\mathbf{x}, \mathbf{a}, \mathbf{w}_i)] = 1$ and $\mathrm{E}[c(\mathbf{x}, \mathbf{a}, \mathbf{w}_i)] = 0$ in case when $\mathbf{a}$ is and is not marked with $\mathbf{w}_i$ respectively. Fingerprint detection is performed using a Neyman-Pearson test $c(\mathbf{x}, \mathbf{a}, \mathbf{w}_i) \lessgtr T$, where the detection threshold T establishes the error probabilities for false positives and negatives. As an example, the adversarial clique $\mathbb{Q}$ may use estimation and collusion via averaging to produce a "clean" copy of the content. Content averaging by a collusion of K users produces a copy $\mathbf{z} = K^{-1} \sum_{i=1}^{K} \mathbf{y}_i$ such that $\mathrm{E}[c(\mathbf{x}, \mathbf{z}, \mathbf{w}_i \in \mathbb{Q})] = K^{-1}$. If we denote the efficacy of fingerprint estimation using

$E[c(\mathbf{x}, \mathbf{e}_i, \mathbf{w}_i)] = \frac{1}{\alpha}$, where $\mathbf{e}_i$ is the attack vector computed via estimation from $\mathbf{y}_i$, then $E[c(\mathbf{x}, K^{-1} \sum_{i=1}^{K}(\mathbf{y}_i - \mathbf{e}_i), \mathbf{w}_i)] = (\alpha K)^{-1}$. Thus, in the asymptotic case, the estimation attack improves the overall effort by the colluders for a scaling factor α. Knowing that collusion resistance of the best fingerprinting codes for 2 hour video sequences is on the order of $K \sim 10^2$ [7, 10], we conclude that estimation is an important component of the overall attack.

Finally, it appears that estimating fingerprints is no different from estimating arbitrary watermarks. However, there exists a strong difference in the way how watermarks for content screening [11] and fingerprinting [4] are designed. The replication that is necessary for watermarks tailored to content screening[1], makes their estimation substantially easier [11]. On the other hand, fingerprints can be designed with almost no redundancy which makes their estimation substantially more difficult. At last, during fingerprint detection, the forensic tool has access to the original which greatly improves the detection rates.

2   Related Work

The idea of watermark removal via estimation is not new. To the best of our knowledge, all developed schemes for the estimation attack have targeted "blindly" detected watermarks. For example, Langelaar et al. used a 3×3 median and 3×3 high pass filters to successfully launch an estimation attack on a spread spectrum image watermarking scheme [12]. Su and Girod used a Wiener filter to estimate arbitrary watermarks; they constructively expanded their attack to provide a power-spectrum condition required for a watermark to resist minimum mean-squared error estimation [13]. Next, Voloshynovskiy et al. achieved partial watermark removal using a filter based on the Maximum a Posteriori (MAP) principle [14]. Finally, Kirovski et al. investigated the security of a direct-sequence spread-spectrum watermarking scheme for audio by statistically analyzing the effect of the estimation attack on their redundant watermark codes [11]. They used the estimation attack of the form:

$$\mathbf{e} = \text{sign}\left[\sum_{j \in J}(x_j + w) \right], \tag{2}$$

where J is a region in the source signal $\mathbf{x}$ marked with the same watermark chip w. This attack can be optimal under a set of assumptions about the watermark and the source signal [11].

In this paper, we propose a simple but novel joint source-fingerprint estimator which performs particularly well on low-frequency watermarks. We also show an interesting anomaly specific to watermarking schemes that construct watermarks dependent upon the source: by applying an attack vector dependent upon the source such as vectors produced by our estimation attack, the probability of false positives may substantially increase in the system compared to additive white gaussian noise of similar magnitude. If discovered and unresolved, this issue renders a forensic technology inapplicable.

---

[1] To resist de-synchronization attacks.

3   A Video Fingerprinting Scheme

In order to present our estimation attack, we use an existing well-engineered video fingerprinting scheme. The scheme is based upon the image watermarking approach presented in [15] and adjusted and improved to video fingerprinting by Harmanci et al. [16, 17, 18]. Their video fingerprinting scheme marks the content by designing a complexity-adaptive watermark signal via solving an optimization problem. The marking process is performed in several steps. First, each frame of the video sequence is transformed into the DWT(Discrete Wavelet Transform) domain. Since watermarks are applied only to the DC sub-bands (the lowest frequency sub-bands), the algorithm packs these coefficients into a 3D prism $x(a, b, t)$, where the third dimension t represents the frame index (i.e., time). Based upon a unique user key, the fingerprint embedding algorithm selects pseudo-randomly, in terms of positions and sizes, a collection of sub-prisms $\mathbb{P} = \{p_1, \ldots, p_n\} \subset x$ that may overlap. Prisms' dimensions are upper and lower bounded (e.g., from $12 \times 16 \times 20$ to $36 \times 48 \times 60$). Then, the coefficients in each prism $p_j \in \mathbb{P}$ are weighted using a smooth weighting prism u_j. The weighting prisms are generated pseudo-randomly using a user-specific secret key. Finally, the algorithm computes first order statistics for each $g(p_j \cdot u_j)$ (e.g., $g()$ computes the mean of its argument) and quantizes them using a private quantizer $q(g(p_j \cdot u_j), \underline{bit})$, where $\underline{bit}$ represents the embedded user-specific data. The desired watermark strength is achieved by adjusting the quantization step size during the embedding. The content update $\Delta_j = q(g(p_j \cdot u_j), \underline{bit}) - g(p_j \cdot u_j)$ is spread among the pixels of the containing prism using an optimization primitive.

To get a better visual quality, Harmanci et al. generate a "complexity map" c using the spatial and temporal information of each component, which is then employed in solving the underlying optimization problem to regularize the watermark. Specifically, the spatial complexity $c_s(a, b, t)$ for a given component in the DWT-DC sub-band is determined by estimating the variance of the coefficients in a $v = M \times M$ 2D window centered at (a, b, t). Typically, $M = 5$. The decision relies on the i.i.d. assumption for the coefficients. Using the Gaussian entropy formula $c_s = \frac{1}{2} \log 2\pi e \sigma^2(v)$, where $\sigma^2()$ denotes argument variance, the algorithm estimates the spatial entropy rate of that component and uses it as a measure of spatial complexity. To determine the temporal complexity c_t, the scheme performs first order auto-regression (AR) analysis with window length L among the corresponding components along the optical flow [19]. The temporal complexity is obtained by applying the Gaussian entropy formula on the distribution of the innovation process of the AR1 model. Then, c_t and c_s are linearly combined to compute c. By employing the "complexity map," the resulting watermark is locally adapted to the statistical complexity of the signal. While aimed at improving the perceptual quality of the resulting sequence, the complexity map significantly reduces the exploration space for watermark estimation.

Based upon the complexity map, the watermark embedding procedure computes the optimal update values for each DWT-DC coefficient that realizes the desired Δ_j for each selected prism p_j. Finally, the scheme applies a low-pass filter both spatially and temporally on the watermark signal to further improve watermark's imperceptibility.

Figure 1 shows an example watermark extracted from a single frame of our test video sequence as well as the frequency spectrum analysis of the watermark. One can notice

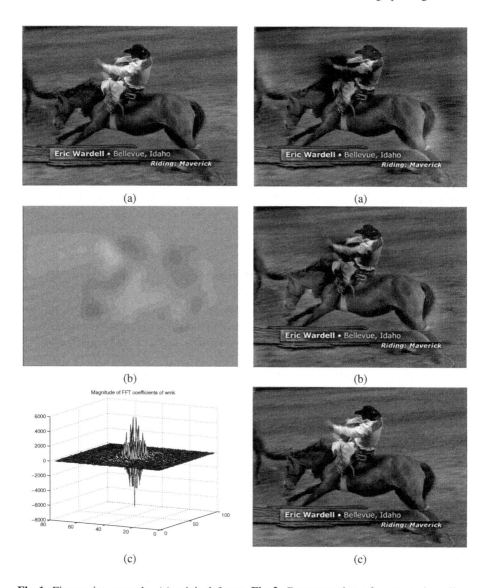

Fig. 1. Fingerprint example: (a) original frame from the benchmark video clip, (b) resulting fingerprint constructed as a marking of this frame – the fingerprint is in the pixel domain, scaled by a factor 10 and shift to a mean of 128, and (c) watermark amplitude in the DFT domain

Fig. 2. Demonstration of perceptual quality: the first frame of the (a) attacked video with $\alpha = 1.5$, (b) attacked video with $\alpha = 1$, and (c) original video

that the effective watermark is highly smoothed and that most of the watermark energy is located in the low-frequency band. This conclusion is important for the application of the estimation attack.

Given a received video signal $\mathbf{z}$, the detector first employs the information of the original video signal to undo the operations such as histogram equalization, rotation, de-synchronization, etc. Next, using a suspect user key, the detector extracts the feature vector in the same way as the embedding process. It employs a correlation based detection to identify the existence of a watermark as follows:

$$\gamma = \frac{(\mathbf{g}_z - \mathbf{g}) \cdot (\hat{\mathbf{g}} - \mathbf{g})}{||\hat{\mathbf{g}} - \mathbf{g}||^2} \lessgtr T, \tag{3}$$

where $\mathbf{g}_z = \{g(\bar{\mathbf{p}}_j \cdot \mathbf{u}_j), j = 1 \ldots n\}$, $\hat{\mathbf{g}} = \{q(g(\mathbf{p}_j \cdot \mathbf{u}_j)), j = 1 \ldots n\}$, and $\mathbf{g} = \{g(\mathbf{p}_j \cdot \mathbf{u}_j), j = 1 \ldots n\}$, and $\bar{\mathbf{p}}_j$ represents a prism extracted from $\mathbf{z}$ at a position that corresponds to the position of $\mathbf{p}_j$ within $\mathbf{x}$. If γ is greater than a certain threshold T, the detector concludes that $\mathbf{z}$ is marked with the fingerprint generated using the suspect user key; otherwise, no fingerprint is detected.

4   Joint Source-Fingerprint Estimation

In this paper, we propose a simple attack with an objective to perform joint source-fingerprint estimation. Based upon the observation that the targeted fingerprints are mainly located in the low-frequency band, we propose a dual-filter attack that is relatively computationally inexpensive and efficient.

The estimation attack is performed in the DWT-DC domain where the fingerprints are embedded. For each coefficient $x(a, b, t)$ in this domain, we choose three prisms $\mathbf{k}_1$, $\mathbf{k}_2$ and $\mathbf{k}_3$, all centered at $x(a, b, t)$. The outer and largest of the prisms, $\mathbf{k}_1$, encompasses the next smaller one, $\mathbf{k}_2 \subset \mathbf{k}_1$. Prism $\mathbf{k}_3$ is smaller than $\mathbf{k}_1$. We average the coefficients inside two 3D regions: inside $\mathbf{k}_3$ and inside $\mathbf{k}_1 - \mathbf{k}_2$. Since both the smoothing and weighting functions are built to maintain in most cases the same sign for the fingerprint over a certain small region in $\mathbf{x}$, we use:

$$\mathbf{e}_3 = \frac{1}{|\mathbf{k}_3|} \sum_{p \in \mathbf{k}_3} [x(p) + w(p)] \tag{4}$$

as the estimate of $\bar{x} + w(a, b, t)$ where $\bar{x}$ denotes the mean of the underlying source. As the targeted fingerprint is a low-frequency signal, we assume that $\text{sign}(w(p))$ is mostly univocal for $p \in \mathbf{k}_3$, thus, $\text{sign}(|\mathbf{k}_3|^{-1} \sum_{p \in \mathbf{k}_3} w(p))$ represents a good estimate of $\text{sign}(w(a, b, t))$. Next, we use:

$$\mathbf{e}_{12} = \frac{1}{|\mathbf{k}_1 - \mathbf{k}_2|} \sum_{p \in \mathbf{k}_1 - \mathbf{k}_2} [x(p) + w(p)] \tag{5}$$

to obtain an alternate estimate of $\bar{x}$ only. The reasoning is that the fingerprint spread in the region $\mathbf{k}_1 - \mathbf{k}_2$, has a variable sign and that it would average itself out in $\mathbf{e}_{12}$. To achieve this goal, the size of $\mathbf{k}_1 - \mathbf{k}_2$ should be large enough. Also, the size of $\mathbf{k}_3$ is chosen to be relatively small to capture the sign of $w(a, b, t)$ and to get a stable $\bar{x}$ inside $\mathbf{k}_3$. Usually, we choose the size of $\mathbf{k}_3$ to be (6,8,10) to (10,12,14); $\mathbf{k}_1$ has size about 4

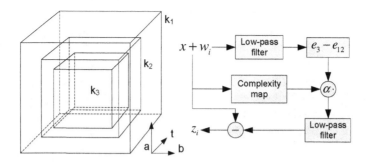

Fig. 3. Diagram of the estimation attack

times as large as $\mathbf{k}_3$; and $\mathbf{k}_2$ is comparable to $\mathbf{k}_3$ or even smaller. Finally, we construct the attack as:

$$\mathbf{z} = \mathbf{x} + \mathbf{w}_i - \alpha\mathbf{c} \cdot (\mathbf{e}_3 - \mathbf{e}_{12}), \tag{6}$$

where α is an amplification factor that can be tuned up as long as $\mathbf{z}$ is acceptably perceptually similar to $\mathbf{x} + \mathbf{w}_i$. In addition, we use a complexity map $\mathbf{c}$ derived prior to the attack to improve the perceptual effect of the attack and thus, maximize α. The procedure for computing the complexity map is described in Section 3. Since most of the watermark is concentrated in the low frequency band, we employ low-pass filter on the watermarked video signal before and after the estimation attack described in Eqn.6. The diagram of the final attack process is illustrated in Figure 3.

5   Experimental Results

In this section, we demonstrate the effectiveness of the proposed estimation attack. In the experiments we choose the "Rodeo Show" video sequence with frame size 640×480 as the host video sequence, and apply the video fingerprinting scheme of [17]. The embedding parameters are chosen to obtain a solid trade-off between perceptual quality and robustness. The deployed fingerprinting scheme is particularly efficient for video sequences with significant "random" motion, thus, the used video sequence is selected to exhibit the best in the marking scheme. We apply the estimation attack using a prism $\mathbf{k}_3$ of size $7 \times 9 \times 11$, a large prism $\mathbf{k}_1$ of size $25 \times 33 \times 81$, and $\mathbf{k}_2 = \emptyset$. We chose $\alpha \in \{0.5, 1, 1.5\}$ to adjust the attack strength for high, medium, and low perceptual fidelity of the resulting video sequence respectively. Figure 2 illustrates the resulting perceptual quality for the attacked signal for $\alpha \in \{1, 1.5\}$ using the first frame of the benchmark video sequence.

We show the results of the estimation attack in Figures 4 and 5. First, we use 50 different keys to create and embed distinct fingerprints into the test video sequence, resulting in 50 unique copies. Then, in each of these copies we perform fingerprint detection using the corresponding key used during fingerprint embedding. Figures 4(a), (b) and (c) represent the histogram of the detection statistic γ for $\alpha = \{1.5, 1, 0.5\}$ respectively. The (mean, variance) for these three histograms are (a): (0.407, 0.214);

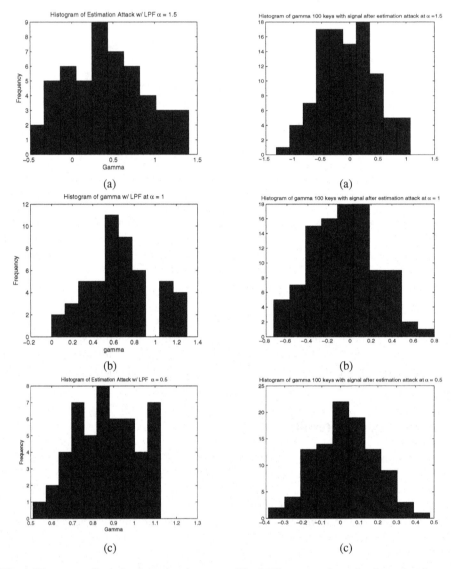

Fig. 4. Histogram of γ under the estimation attack for different α in the case of detecting using the same key as embedding: (a) $\alpha = 1.5$, (b) $\alpha = 1$, (c) $\alpha = 0.5$

Fig. 5. Histogram of γ under the estimation attack for different α in the case of detecting using a different key as embedding: (a) $\alpha = 1.5$, (b) $\alpha = 1$, (c) $\alpha = 0.5$

(b): $(0.661, 0.095)$; (c): $(0.866, 0.023)$. From the results, we can observe that due to the estimation attack, the mean of γ significantly deviates from $\gamma = 1$ (the expected value when there is no attack) and the deviation increases for large α. On the average, approximately 60% and 35% of the fingerprint correlation is removed after applying the estimation attack with $\alpha = \{1.5, 1\}$ respectively. More importantly, the variance of the

γ statistic becomes relatively large, e.g., the range of γ for $\alpha = 1.5$ covers $\{-0.5, 1.3\}$. Compared to additive white gaussian noise (AWGN) of the same magnitude as our estimation attack, which will be shown later, the fingerprint detector experiences a nearly 12-fold (from $\sigma^2(\gamma) = 0.0175$ to 0.2136) and 19-fold (from $\sigma^2(\gamma) = 0.0050$ to 0.0951) increase in the variance of the detection statistic γ for $\alpha = \{1.5, 1\}$ respectively. We use this observation to point to a significant anomaly of the particular fingerprinting scheme [17].

According to [16, 17, 18], the examined fingerprinting scheme has been tested under various attacks. It was reported that after the MCTF(Motion Compensated Temporal Filtering) attack with various filter lengthes, the detection statistic γ ranges from 0.85 to 1. Thus the fingerprint can be detected with high probability. Other attacks such as rotation by 2 degrees, cropping by 10%, and the MPEG2 compression at bit rate 500kpbs result in the detection statistic γ around 1 and range within [0.6, 1.4] [16, 17]. A general estimation attack based on Wiener filtering similar to the one in [13] was proposed and examined in [15], where the watermark can be detected without an error. Compared with these non-content dependent attacks, the proposed attack is more effective in removing the watermark.

In the second set of experiments, we examine the scenario when a fingerprint is created and embedded using a key i and detected with a different key j. This test aims at estimating the probability of a false positive under attack, a feature of crucial importance for fingerprinting systems. A solid fingerprinting scheme must observe low probability of false positives for both cases: when detection is done on $\mathbf{x} + \mathbf{w}_i$ as well as $f(\mathbf{x} + \mathbf{w}_i)$. Function $f()$ represents an arbitrary attack procedure that does not have knowledge of the user keys. According to [16], the detection statistic γ with incorrect detection key ranges within [-0.02, 0.02]. However, from Figure 5, one can observe that the proposed estimation attack increases the variance of γ so that non-trivial portion of the keys results in γ as high as 0.8 or even 1. Compared to additive white gaussian noise (AWGN) of the same magnitude as our estimation attack, the fingerprint detector experiences a nearly 14-fold (from $\sigma(\gamma)^2 = 0.0175$ to 0.2418) and 20-fold (from $\sigma(\gamma)^2 = 0.0050$ to 0.1008) increase in the variance of the detection statistic γ for $\alpha = \{1.5, 1\}$ respectively. Since the tail of the gaussian error function is proportional to $\sqrt{N}/\sigma(\gamma)$, in order to maintain the same level of false positives as in the case of detecting a fingerprint on the attacked $\mathbf{x} + \mathbf{w}_i$, the detector must consume $10 \sim 20$ times more samples to produce equivalent error rates. We were not able to understand analytically the unexpected increase in false positives under the estimation attack – however, we speculate that the dependency of watermarks with respect to the source (content-dependent watermarking) has made them prone to attack vectors which are also content-dependent.

To further demonstrate the effectiveness of the proposed estimation attack, we apply the AWGN attack with the same energy as introduced by the estimation attacks. We choose $\alpha = 1.5$ as an example. In Figure 6(a) and (b), we show the histogram of γ for the case of "same-key" and "different-key" detection, respectively. The increase of the variance is far less significant than that incurred by the estimation attack. Figure 6(c) shows the visual quality of the AWGN-attacked frame, from which we can see that the distortion introduced by AWGN is more noticeable than that introduced

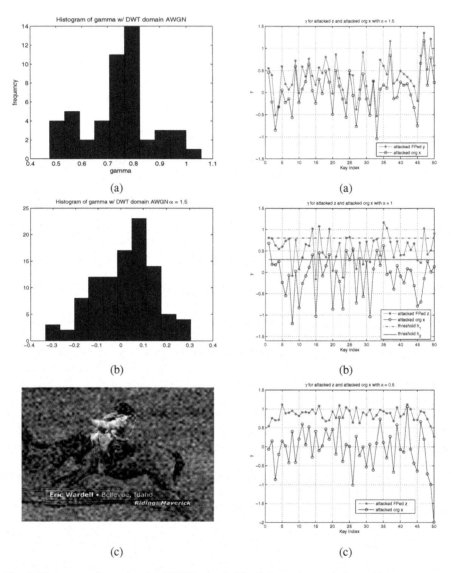

Fig. 6. Histogram of γ under the AWGN attack with equivalent energy as the estimation attack for $\alpha = 1.5$: (a) detecting with the same key as embedding; (b) detecting with a different key as embedding; (c) frame after the AWGN attack

Fig. 7. Detection statistic γ with respect to various keys for attacked signal $\hat{z}$ and attacked original signal $\hat{x}$: (a) $\alpha = 0.5$; (b) $\alpha = 1$; (c) $\alpha = 1.5$

by the estimation attack. Comparison of the probability of error and visual quality between the estimation and AWGN attacks, demonstrates that the proposed attack successfully captures the content-based watermark and is a far-stronger attack than the "blind" AWGN attack.

6   Discussions and Countermeasure

As can be seen from the experimental results, the power of the proposed attack lies in the introduced high probability of false positive P_{fp}. To better understand this effect, we also examine the detection performance after applying the estimation attack directly onto original signal $\mathbf{x}$ and detecting it with various keys. The results are shown in Figure 7 along with the detection of the attacked signal $\hat{\mathbf{z}} = f(\mathbf{x}+\mathbf{w}_i)$ using corresponding key i. The estimation strength α for Figure 7(a) (b) and (c) are chosen to be 1.5, 1 and 0.5 respectively. The results clearly show that the high false positive probability in detection comes from the fact that the attacked original signal $\hat{\mathbf{x}}$ is highly correlated with the fingerprints generated from many keys. The underlying reason is that the estimation process on the original signal estimates the low frequency information from the $\mathbf{x}$. On the other hand, each fingerprint is built to be content related and has gone through an intensive low-pass filtering process in the addressed video fingerprinting scheme [17]. As a result, the fingerprint mainly contains the low frequency information of $\mathbf{x}$ and thus highly correlated with the $\hat{\mathbf{x}}$, which leads to a large value of false positive probability P_{fp}.

Now considering from the embedder's perspective, we try to find ways to combat this estimation attack. From Figure 7 we see that the detection statistic γ is key-dependent, i.e. for some keys, the γ for the attacked original signal $\hat{\mathbf{x}}$ is high, while for others the γ is low. Since the embedder has the freedom to choose secret keys for embedding, he can leverage on this freedom to deploy a countermeasure by using only the key set that results in low P_{fp}. Specifically, the embedder can first examine a large set of keys and then choose those keys that have high γ on $\hat{\mathbf{z}}$ while have low γ on $\hat{\mathbf{x}}$. The embedder can define two thresholds h_1 and h_2, according to the desired P_{fn} and P_{fp} respectively, to help the sifting process as shown in Figure 7(b). The keys whose γ on $\hat{\mathbf{z}}$ is higher than h_1 and γ on $\hat{\mathbf{x}}$ is lower than h_2 are eligible for embedding. Other keys may result in high P_{fp} or P_{fn} and will be discarded. In the example shown in Figure 7 (b), only 36th, 47th and 50th keys are eligible for embedding given $h_1 = 0.8$ and $h_2 = 0.3$.

This countermeasure is quite straight forward and requires a significant amount of computations to select the key set. Moreover, the number of eligible keys are quite limited, e.g. only 3 out of 50 keys in Figure 7(b) satisfy the condition of h_1 and h_2. Thus, to get a certain number of eligible keys, the embedder has to examine a large pool of keys. This may not be feasible for real applications such as fingerprinting a 2-hour movie signal. The results suggest that introducing low-frequency content-based signal as fingerprint is vulnerable to the estimation type of attack, which should be taken into consideration in the fingerprint design.

7   Conclusions

We proposed a simple dual-filter estimator that aims at removing low-frequency fingerprints embedded in video signals. Although we construct an instance of the attack and show its efficacy using a specific video fingerprinting algorithm, the generic form of the attack can be applied to an arbitrary video marking scheme. In the conducted experiments, the attack procedure on the average removed a substantial portion of the embedded fingerprints compared to additive white gaussian noise. To the best of our knowledge, the attack is the first in published literature to induce a substantial increase of false positives in a particular fingerprinting scheme as opposed to a "blind" attack.

Acknowledgment

We thank Dr. M.K. Mihcak and Dr. Y. Yacobi for the valuable discussions.

References

1. I. Cox, J. Kilian, F. Leighton, and T. Shamoon, "Secure Spread Spectrum Watermarking for Multimedia", *IEEE Trans. on Image Processing*, 6(12), pp.1673–1687, 1997.
2. F.A.P. Petitcolas, R.J. Anderson, and M.G. Kuhn. "Attacks on Copyright Marking Systems". *Info Hiding Workshop*, pp.218–238, 1998.
3. F. Ergun, J. Kilian and R. Kumar, "A Note on the limits of Collusion-Resistant Watermarks", *Eurocrypt '99*, 1999.
4. D. Schonberg and D. Kirovski. "Fingerprinting and Forensic Analysis of Multimedia". *ACM Multimedia*, pp.788-795, 2004.
5. D. Boneh and J. Shaw, "Collusion-secure Fingerprinting for Digital Data", *IEEE Tran. on Information Theory*, 44(5), pp.1897-1905, 1998.
6. Y. Yacobi, "Improved Boneh-Shaw Content Fingerprinting", *CT-RSA 2001, LNCS 2020*, pp.378-391, 2001.
7. W. Trappe, M. Wu, Z.J. Wang, and K.J.R. Liu, "Anti-collusion Fingerprinting for Multimedia", *IEEE Trans. on Sig. Proc.*, 51(4), pp.1069-1087, 2003.
8. Z.J. Wang, M. Wu, H. Zhao, W. Trappe, and K.J.R. Liu, "Anti-Collusion Forensics of Multimedia Fingerprinting Using Orthogonal Modulation", *IEEE Trans. on Image Proc.*, pp. 804–821, June 2005.
9. S. He and M. Wu, "Joint Coding and Embedding Techniques for Multimedia Fingerprinting," *IEEE Trans. on Info. Forensics and Security*, Vol.1, No.2, pp.231–247, June 2006.
10. D. Kirovski. "Collusion of Fingerprints via the Gradient Attack". *IEEE International Symposium on Information Theory*, 2005.
11. D. Kirovski and H.S. Malvar. "Spread Spectrum Watermarking of Audio Signals". *IEEE Transactions on Signal Processing*, Vol.51, No.4, pp.1020-33, 2003.
12. G. Langelaar, R. Lagendijk, and J. Biemond. "Removing Spatial Spread Spectrum Watermarks by Non-linear Filtering". *Proceedings of European Signal Processing Conference (EUSIPCO 1998)*, Vol.4, pp.2281–2284, 1998.
13. J. Su and B. Girod. "Power Spectrum Condition for L2-efficient Watermarking". *IEEE Proc. of International Conference on Image Processing (ICIP 1999)*, 1999.
14. S. Voloshynovskiy, S. Pereira, A. Herrigel, N. Baumgrtner, and T. Pun. "Generalized watermarking attack based on watermark estimation and perceptual remodulation". *SPIE Conference on Security and Watermarking of Multimedia Content II*, 2000.
15. M.K. Mihcak, R. Venkatesan, and M. Kesal. "Watermarking via Optimization Algorithms for Quantizing Randomized Statistics of Image Regions". *Allerton Conference on Communications, Computing and Control*, 2002.
16. M. Kucukgoz, O. Harmanci, M.K. Mihcak, and R. Venkatesan. "Robust Video Watermarking via Optimization Algorithm for Quantization of Pseudo-Random Semi-Global Statistics". *SPIE Conference on Security, Watermarking and Stegonography*, San Jose, CA, 2005.

17. O. Harmanci and M.K. Mihcak. " Complexity-Regularized Video Watermarking via Quantization of Pseudo-Random Semi-Global Linear Statistics". *Proceedings of European Signal Processing Conference (EUSIPCO)*, 2005.
18. O. Harmanci and M.K. Mihcak. "Motion Picture Watermarking Via Quantization of Pseudo-Random Linear Statistics". *Visual Communications and Image Processing Conference*, 2005.
19. S.B. Kang, M. Uyttendaele, S.A.J. Winder, and R. Szeliski. "High Dynamic Range Video", *ACM Trans. on Graphics*, Vol.22, Issue 3, pp.319–325, 2003.

Statistics- and Spatiality-Based Feature Distance Measure for Error Resilient Image Authentication

Shuiming Ye[1,2], Qibin Sun[1], and Ee-Chien Chang[2]

[1] Institute for Infocomm Research, A*STAR, Singapore, 119613
[2] School of Computing, National University of Singapore, Singapore, 117543
{Shuiming, Qibin}@i2r.a-star.edu.sg, Changec@comp.nus.edu.sg

Abstract. Content-based image authentication typically assesses authenticity based on a distance measure between the image to be tested and its original. Commonly employed distance measures such as the Minkowski measures (including Hamming and Euclidean distances) may not be adequate for content-based image authentication since they do not exploit statistical and spatial properties in features. This paper proposes a feature distance measure for content-based image authentication based on statistical and spatial properties of the feature differences. The proposed statistics- and spatiality-based measure (SSM) is motivated by an observation that most malicious manipulations are localized whereas acceptable manipulations result in global distortions. A statistical measure, kurtosis, is used to assess the shape of the feature difference distribution; a spatial measure, the maximum connected component size, is used to assess the degree of object concentration of the feature differences. The experimental results have confirmed that our proposed measure is better than previous measures in distinguishing malicious manipulations from acceptable ones.

Keywords: Feature Distance Measure, Image Authentication, Image Transmission, Error Concealment, Digital Watermarking, Digital Signature.

1 Introduction

With the wide availability of digital cameras and image processing software, the generation and manipulation of digital images are easy now. To protect the trustworthiness of digital images, image authentication techniques are required in many scenarios, for example, applications in health care.

Image authentication, in general, differs from data authentication in cryptography. Data authentication is designed to detect a single bit change whereas image authentication aims to authenticate the content but not the specific data representation of an image [1], [2]. Therefore, image manipulations which do not change semantic meaning are often acceptable, such as contrast adjustment, histogram equalization, and compression [3], [4]. Lossy transmission is also considered as acceptable since errors under certain level in images would be tolerable

Y.Q. Shi (Eds.): Transactions on DHMS II, LNCS 4499, pp. 48–67, 2007.

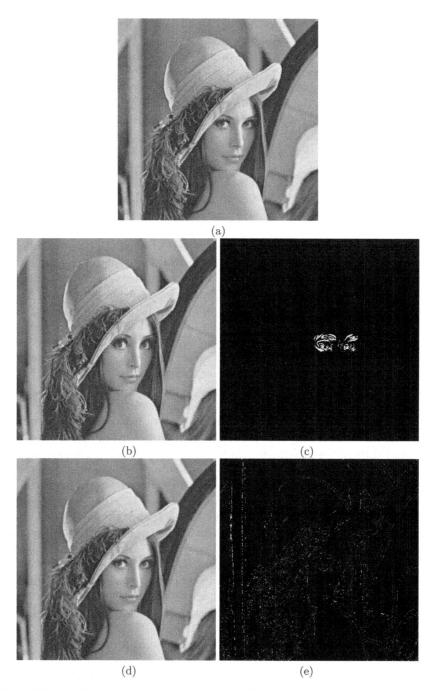

Fig. 1. Discernable patterns of edge feature differences caused by acceptable image manipulation and malicious modification: (a) original image; (b) tampered image; (c) feature difference of (b); (d) blurred image (by Gaussian 3×3 filter); (e) feature difference of (d)

and acceptable [5]. Other manipulations that modify image content are classified as malicious manipulations, such as object removal or insertion. Image authentication is desired to be robust to acceptable manipulations, and necessary to be sensitive to malicious ones.

In order to be robust to acceptable manipulations, several content-based image authentication schemes have been proposed [6], [7], [8]. These schemes may be robust to one or several specific manipulations, however, they would classify the image damaged by transmission errors as unauthentic [9]. Furthermore, content-based image authentication typically measures authenticity in terms of the distance between a feature vector from the received image and its corresponding vector from the original image, and compares the distance with a preset threshold to make a decision [10], [11]. Commonly employed distance measures, such as the Minkowski metrics [12] (including Hamming and Euclidean distances), may not be suitable for robust image authentication. The reason is that even if these measures are the same (e.g., we cannot tell whether the question image is authentic or not), the feature difference patterns under typical acceptable modifications or malicious ones may be still distinguishable (feature differences are differences between the feature extracted from the original image and the feature extracted from the testing image). That is to say, these measures do not properly exploit statistical or spatial properties of image features. For example, the Hamming distance measures of Fig. 1(b) and Fig. 1(d) are almost the same, but yet, one could argue that Fig. 1(b) is probably distorted by malicious tampering since the feature differences concentrate on the eyes.

The objective of this paper is to propose a distance measure based on statistical and spatial properties of the feature differences for content-based image authentication. The proposed measure is derived by exploiting the discernable patterns of feature differences between the original image and the distorted image to distinguish acceptable manipulations from malicious ones. Two properties, the kurtosis of the feature difference distribution and the maximum connected component size in the feature differences, are combined to evaluate the discernable patterns. We call the proposed measure statistics- and spatiality-based measure (SSM) since it considers both global statistical properties and spatial properties. Many acceptable manipulations, which were detected as malicious modifications by previous schemes based on Minkowski metrics, were correctly verified by the proposed scheme based on SSM. To illustrate how the proposed SSM can improve the performance of image authentication scheme, we applied it in a semi-fragile image authentication scheme [13] to authenticate images damaged by transmission errors. The proposed error resilient scheme obtained better robustness against transmission errors in JPEG or JPEG2000 images and other acceptable manipulations than the scheme proposed in [13].

2   Proposed Statistics- and Spatiality-Based Measure (SSM) for Image Authentication

Content-based or feature-based image authentication generally verifies authenticity by comparing the distance between the feature vector extracted from the testing image and the original with some preset thresholds [14]. The distance metric commonly used is the Minkowski metric $d(X, Y)$ [12]:

$$d(X, Y) = (\sum_{i=1}^{N} |x_i - y_i|^r)^{1/r} \tag{1}$$

where X, Y are two N dimensional feature vectors, and r is a Minkowski factor. Note that when r is set as 2, it is actually Euclidean distance; when r is 1, Manhattan distance (or Hamming distance for binary vectors).

However, the Minkowski metric does not exploit statistical or spatial properties of image features. Therefore, the image authentication scheme based on Minkowski metric may not be suitable to distinguish the tampered images (e.g., small local objects removed or modified) from the images by acceptable manipulations such as lossy compression. On the other hand, we found that even if the Minkowski metric distances are the same, the feature difference under typical acceptable manipulations and malicious ones are still distinguishable especially in the case that the feature contains spatial information such as edges or block DCT coefficients. Therefore, the Minkowski metric is not a proper measure for content-based image authentication.

2.1   Main Observations of Feature Differences

Many features used in content-based image authentication are composed of localized information about the image such as edges [3], [6], block DCT coefficients [1], [10], [13], highly compressed version of the original image [7], or block intensity histogram [11]. To facilitate discussions, we let x_i be the feature value at spatial location i, and X be an N-dimension feature vector, for example, $N = W \cdot H$ when using edge feature (W and H are the width and height of the image). We define the feature difference vector δ as the difference between feature vector X of the testing image and feature vector Y of the original image:

$$\delta_i = |x_i - y_i| \tag{2}$$

where δ_i is the difference of features at spatial location i.

After examining many discernable feature difference patterns from various image manipulations, we could draw three observations on feature differences:

1. The feature differences by most acceptable operations are evenly distributed spatially, whereas the differences by malicious operations are locally concentrated.
2. The maximum connected component size of the feature differences caused by acceptable manipulations is usually small, whereas the one by malicious operation is large.
3. Even if the maximum connected component size is fairly small, the image could have also been tampered with if those small components are spatially concentrated.

These observations are supported by our intensive experiments and other literatures mentioned previously [6], [9]. Image contents are typically represented by objects and each object is usually represented by spatially clustered image pixels. Therefore, the feature to represent the content of the image would inherit some spatial relations.

A malicious manipulation of an image is usually concentrated on modifying objects in image, changing the image to a new one which carries different visual meaning to the observers. If the contents of an image are modified, the features around the objects may also be changed, and the affected feature points tend to be connected with each other. Therefore, the feature differences introduced by a meaningful tampering typically would be spatially concentrated.

On the contrary, acceptable image manipulations such as image compression, contrast adjustment, and histogram equalization introduce distortions globally into the image. The feature differences may likely to cluster around all objects in the image, therefore they are not as concentrated locally as those by malicious manipulations. In addition, many objects may spread out spatially in the image, thus the feature differences are likely to be evenly distributed with little connectedness. The distortion introduced by transmission errors would also be evenly distributed since the transmission errors are randomly introduced into the image [18].

The above observations not only prove the unsuitability of Minkowski metric to be used in image authentication, but also provide some hints on how a good distance function would work: it should exploit the statistical and spatial properties of feature differences. These observations further lead us to design a new feature distance measure for content-based image authentication.

2.2   Proposed Feature Distance Measure for Image Authentication

Based on the observations discussed so far, a feature distance measure is proposed in this section for image authentication. The distance measure is based on the differences of the two feature vectors from the testing image and from the original image. Two measures are used to exploit statistical and spatial properties of feature differences, including the kurtosis ($kurt$) of feature difference distribution and the maximum connected component size ($mccs$) in the feature difference map. Observation (1) motivates the uses of the kurtosis measure, and observation (2) motivates the uses of the $mccs$ measure. They are combined together since any one of the above alone is still insufficient, as stated in observation (3).

The proposed Statistics- and Spatiality-based Measure (SSM) is calculated by sigmoid membership function based on both $mccs$ and $kurt$. Given two feature vectors X and Y, the proposed feature distance measure $SSM(X, Y)$ is defined as follows:

$$SSM(X,Y) = \frac{1}{1 + e^{\,\alpha(mccs \cdot kurt \cdot \theta^{-2} - \beta)}} \qquad (3)$$

The measure $SSM(X, Y)$ is derived from the feature difference vector δ defined in Eq. (2). The $mccs$ and $kurt$ are obtained from δ, and their details are given in the next few paragraphs. θ is a normalizing factor.

The parameter α controls the changing speed especially at the point $mccs \cdot kurt \cdot \theta^{-2} = \beta$. β is the average $mccs \cdot kurt \cdot \theta^{-2}$ value obtained by calculating from a set of malicious attacked images and acceptable manipulated images. In this paper, the acceptable manipulations are defined as contrast adjustment, noise addition, blurring, sharpening, compression and lossy transmission (with error concealment); the malicious tampering operations are object replacement, addition or removal. During authentication, if the measure $SSM(X, Y)$ of an image is smaller than 0.5 (that is, $mccs \cdot kurt \cdot \theta^{-2} < \beta$, the image is identified as authentic, otherwise it is unauthentic.

Kurtosis. Kurtosis describes the shape of a random variable's probability distribution based on the size of the distribution's tails. It is a statistical measure used to describe the concentration of data around the mean. A high kurtosis portrays a distribution with fat tails and a low even distribution, whereas a low kurtosis portrays a distribution with skinny tails and a distribution concentrated towards the mean.

Therefore, it could be used to distinguish feature difference distribution of the malicious manipulations from that of the acceptable manipulations.

Let us partition the spatial locations of the image into neighborhoods, and let N_i be the i-th neighborhood. That is, N_i is a set of locations that are in a same neighborhood. For example, by dividing the image into blocks of 8×8, we have a total of $W \cdot H/64$ neighborhoods, and each neighborhood contains 64 locations. Let D_i be the total feature distortion in the i-th neighborhood N_i:

$$D_i = \sum_{j \in N_i} \delta_j \tag{4}$$

We can view D_i as a sample of a distribution D. The $kurt$ in the Eq. (3) is the kurtosis of the distribution D. It can be estimated by:

$$kurt(D) = \frac{\sum_{i=1}^{N} (D_i - \mu)^4}{Num\ \sigma^4} - 3 \tag{5}$$

where Num is the total number of all samples used for estimation. μ and σ is the estimated mean and standard deviation of D, respectively.

Maximum Connected Component Size. Connected component is a set of points in which every point is connected to all others. Its size is defined as the total number of points in this set. The maximum connected component size ($mccs$) is usually calculated by morphological operators. The isolated points in the feature difference map are first removed and then broken segments are joined by morphological dilation. The maximum connected component size ($mccs$) is then calculated by using connected components labeling on the feature map based on 8-connected neighborhood. Details can be found in [15].

Normalizing Factor. Since images may have different number of objects, details as well as dimensions, normalization is therefore needed. Instead of using traditional normalization (i.e., the ratios of the number of extracted feature points to image dimension), we employ a new normalizing factor θ as:

$$\theta = \frac{\mu}{W \cdot H} \tag{6}$$

where W and H are the width and height of the image respectively. μ is the estimated mean of D, same as that in Eq.(5). The normalized factor θ makes the proposed measure more suitable for natural scene images.

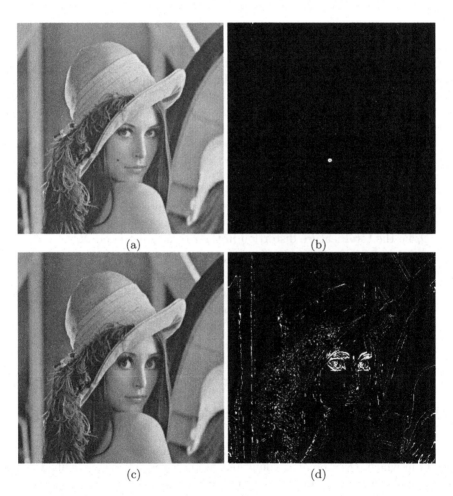

Fig. 2. Cases that required both *mccs* and *kurt* to work together to successfully detect malicious modifications: (a) small object tampered (*kurt*: large; *mccs*: small); (b) feature differences of (a); (c) large object tampered with global distortions (*kurt*: small; *mccs*: large); (d) feature differences of (c)

It is worth noting that the two measures *mccs* and *kurt* should be combined together to handle different malicious tampering. Usually tampering results in three cases in terms of the values of *mccs* and *kurt*: (1) the most general case is that tampered areas are with large maximum connected size and distributed locally (Fig. 1(b)). In this case, both *kurt* and *mccs* are large; (2) small local object is modified such as a small spot added in face (Fig. 2(a)). In this case, the *mccs* is usually very small, but *kurt* is large; (3) tampered areas are with large maximum connected size but these areas are evenly distributed in the whole image (Fig. 2(c)). In this case, the *mccs* is usually large, but *kurt* is small. Therefore, it is necessary for *SSM* to combine these two measures so that *SSM* could detect all these cases of malicious modifications.

3 Application of *SSM* to Error Resilient Image Authentication

Image transmission is always affected by the errors due to channel noises, fading, multi-path transmission and Doppler frequency shift [16] in wireless channel, or packet loss due to congestion in Internet [17]. Therefore, error resilient image authentication which is robust to acceptable manipulations and transmission errors is desirable. Based on the proposed feature distance measure, an error resilient image authentication scheme is proposed in this section.

The proposed error resilient scheme exploits the proposed measure in a generic semi-fragile image authentication framework [8] to distinguish images distorted by transmission errors from maliciously modified ones. The experimental results support that the proposed feature distance measure can improve the performance of the previous scheme in terms of robustness and sensitivity.

3.1 Feature Extraction for Error Resilient Image Authentication

One basic requirement for selecting feature for content-based image authentication is that the feature should be sensitive to malicious attacks on the image content. Edge-based features would be a good choice because usually malicious tampering will incur the changes on edges. And edge may also be robust to some distortions. For instances, the results in [18] show that high edge preserving ratios can be achieved even if there are uncorrectable transmission errors. Therefore, the remaining issue is to make the edge more robust to the defined acceptable manipulations. Note that this is main reason why we employ the normalization by Eq. (6) to suppress those "acceptable" distortions around edges.

In [19], a method based on fuzzy reasoning is proposed to classify each pixel of a gray-value image into a shaped, textured, or smooth feature point. In this paper we adopt their fuzzy reasoning based detector because of its good robustness.

3.2 Image Signing

The image signing procedure is outlined in Fig. 3. Binary edge of the original image is extracted using the fuzzy reasoning based edge detection method [19].

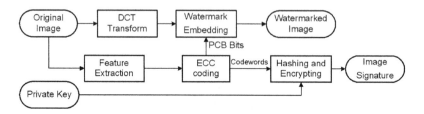

Fig. 3. Signing process of the proposed error resilient image authentication scheme

Then, the edge feature is divided into 8×8 blocks, and edge point number in each block is encoded by error correcting code (ECC) [8]. BCH(7,4,1) is used to generate one parity check bit (PCB) for ECC codeword (edge point number) of every 8×8 block. The signature is generated by hashing and encrypting the concatenated ECC codewords using a private key. Finally, the PCB bits embedded into the DCT coefficients of the image. In our implementation, the PCB bits are embedded into the middle-low frequency DCT coefficients using the same quantization based watermarking as in [13].

Let the total selected DCT coefficients form a set $\mathbf{P}$. For each coefficient c in $\mathbf{P}$, it is replaced with c_w which is calculated by:

$$c_w = \begin{cases} Qround(c/Q), \text{ if } LSB(round(c/Q)) = w \\ Q\left(round(c/Q) + sgn\left(c - Qround(c/Q)\right)\right), \text{ else} \end{cases} \quad (7)$$

where w (0 or 1) is the bit to be embedded. Function $round(x)$ returns the nearest integrate of x, $sgn(x)$ returns the sign of x, and $LSB(x)$ returns the least significant bit of x. Eq. (7) makes sure that the LSB of the coefficient is the same as the watermark bit.

Note that embedding procedure should not affect the feature extracted, since the watermarking procedure would introduce some distortions. In order to exclude the effect of watermarking from feature extraction, a compensation operator C_w is adopted before feature extraction and watermarking:

$$\begin{cases} I_c = C_w(I) \\ I_w = f_e(I_c) \end{cases} \quad (8)$$

$$C_w(I) = IDCT\left\{IntQuan\left(d_i, 2Q, \mathbf{P}\right)\right\} \quad (9)$$

where d_i is the i-th DCT coefficient of I, and IDCT is inverse DCT transform. $f_e(I)$ is the watermarking function, and I_w is the final watermarked image. The IntQuan(c, $\mathbf{P}$, Q) function is defined as:

$$IntQuan\left(c, Q, \mathbf{P}\right) = \begin{cases} c, \text{ if } c \notin \mathbf{P} \\ Q\,round(c/Q), \text{ else} \end{cases} \quad (10)$$

C_w is designed according to the watermarking algorithm, which uses $2Q$ to pre-quantize the DCT coefficients before feature extraction and watermarking. That is, from Eq. (7), (9) and (10), we can get $C_w(I_w) = C_w(I)$, thus $f_e(I_w) = f_e(I)$, i.e., the feature extracted from the original image I is the same as the one from the watermarked image I_w. This compensation operator ensures that watermarking does not affect the extracted feature.

3.3   Image Authenticity Verification

The image verification procedure can be viewed as an inverse process of the image signing procedure, as shown in Fig. 4. Firstly, error concealment is carried out if transmission errors are detected. The feature of image is extracted using the same method as used in image signing procedure. Watermarks are then extracted. If there are no uncorrectable errors in ECC codewords, the authentication is based on bit-wise comparison between the decrypted hashed feature and the hashed feature extracted from the image [8]. Otherwise, image authenticity is calculated by the *SSM* based on differences between the PCB bits of the re-extracted feature and the extracted watermark. Finally, if the image is identified as unauthentic, the attacked areas are then detected.

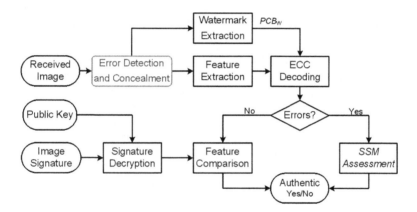

Fig. 4. Image authentication process of the proposed error resilient image authentication scheme

Error Concealment. Given an image to be verified, the first step is to conceal the errors if some transmission errors are detected. For wavelet-based images, edge directed filter-based error concealment algorithm proposed in [18] is adopted. For DCT-based JPEG images, a content-based error concealment proposed in [20] is used.

It is efficient and advisable to apply error concealment before image authentication since the edge feature of the error-concealed image is much closer to the original one than that of the damaged image [18], [20]. As a result, the content authenticity of the error concealed image is higher than that of the damaged image, which is validated in our experiments of the error resilient image authentication.

Image Content Authenticity. Given an image to be verified, we repeat feature extraction described in image signing procedure. The corresponding PCB bits (PCB_W) of all 8×8 blocks (one bit/block) of the image are extracted from the embedded watermarks. Then the feature set extracted from the image is combined with the corresponding PCBs to form ECC codewords. If all codewords are correctable, we concatenate all codewords and cryptographically hash the result sequence. The final authentication result is then concluded by bit-by-bit comparison between these two hashed sets. If there are uncorrectable errors in ECC codewords, image authenticity is calculated based on the proposed distance measure. The two feature vectors in the proposed measure are PCB_W from watermarks and the recalculated PCB bits (PCB_F) from ECC coding of the re-extracted image feature set. If the distance measure between PCB_W and PCB_F is smaller than 0.5 ($SSM(PCB_W, PCB_F) < 0.5$), the image is authentic. Otherwise, the image is unauthentic.

Feature Aided Attack Location. If the image is verified as unauthentic, the tampered areas will be detected. Attack location is an important part of the authentication result since the detected attacked areas give the users a clear figure where the image has been possibly tampered with. The diagram of our feature aided attack location algorithm is shown in Fig. 5. The attack areas are detected using information from watermarks and image feature. The difference map between PCB_W and PCB_F is calculated, and then morphological operations are used to compute connected areas, with isolated pixels and small connected areas removed. After these operations, the difference map is masked with the union of the watermark and feature. The masking operation can refine the detected areas by concentrating them on the objects in the tampered image or in the original image. The areas in the difference map which do not belong to any object (defined by edge feature) are removed, which may be a false alarm of some noises.

It is worth noting that the authentication result of our scheme is friendly to users. Since human perceptivity treats image as a combination of objects, some objects may be region of interest (ROI) to users. If the image fails to pass the authentication, our scheme provides possible attacked areas which concentrate on objects. If these detected areas are not the user's ROI, further decision can be

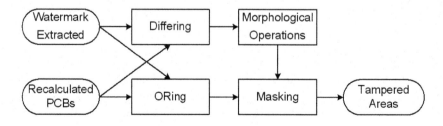

Fig. 5. Feature aided attack location process

made by the user on a case by case basis. Finally, this scheme can also provide a degree of authenticity (by *SSM* measure) to the user which gives the user a confidence on the trustiness of the image.

4   Experimental Results and Discussions

In this Section, the proposed *SSM* is evaluated by experiments, compared with Minkowski metrics and our previous results [13]. In our experiments, JPEG and JPEG2000 image formats were used. Testing images include *Actor, Barbara, Bike, Airplane, Fruits, Girl, Goldhill, Lena, Mandrill, Monarch, Pepper, Woman*, and so on. The dimensions of these images differ among 512×512, 640×512, 640×800, and 720×576. *Daubechies* 9/7 wavelet filter is used for the wavelet transformation which is used in JPEG2000 standard [21]. The parameters α and β in Eq.(3) were set to 0.5 and 48.0, respectively.

4.1   Feature Distance Measure Evaluation

The observations present in Section 2, which are the basis of the proposed *SSM*, were investigated first in our experiments. Edge detected by [19] was selected as feature in our evaluations. Fig. 6 shows the histogram of edge difference and their respective probability density estimates of noisy, error concealed, damaged and maliciously tampered images. We can find that the distribution of feature differences between malicious tampered image and the original image have a much longer tail than that of the error-concealed image. The damaged, error-concealed and noisy images all have smaller right tails. These results support our observations that the maliciously tampered image has a different pattern of feature differences from that of the acceptable manipulations.

Some acceptable distortions and malicious attacks were introduced into the original images for robustness evaluation. The proposed *SSM* was compared with *Hamming* (Minkowski Metric with $r=1$ for binary feature) as shown in Fig. 7.

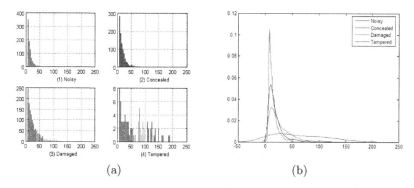

(a)   (b)

Fig. 6. Different patterns of edge difference distribution: (a) histograms of edge differences; (b) probability density estimation

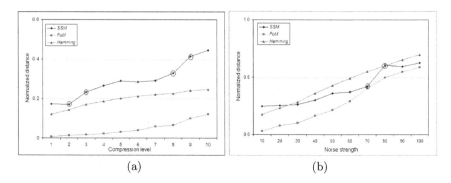

(a)   (b)

Fig. 7. Distance measures comparison: (a) for JPEG compressions (b) for *Gaussian* noises

Pratt's *Figure of Merit* (*FoM*) [22] was also used for comparison, since it is commonly used at measuring image similarity based on edges, which is defined as:

$$FoM = \frac{1}{\max(N_O, N_C)} \sum_{i=1}^{N_C} \frac{1}{1 + \lambda \times di^2} \qquad (11)$$

where N_C and N_O are the number of detected and original edge pixels, respectively. d_i is the *Euclidean* distance between the detected edge pixel and the nearest original edge pixel, and λ is a constant typically set to 0.1. Fig. 7(a) shows the experimental results of the proposed *SSM* for image *Lena* after JPEG compression, and Fig. 7(b) shows the experimental results for Gaussian noisy images. These figures show that the *Hamming* and *FoM* distances are almost linear to the compression level or Gaussian noise strength. On the contrary, there were some sharper changes (such as the circled points in Fig. 7) in *SSM* curves which may be good choices for authenticity threshold. As an image can be considered as points in a continuous space, it is typically difficult to set up a sharp boundary between authentic and unauthentic images [10]. This intrinsic fuzziness makes the content-based authentication design challenging and, likely, ad hoc in most cases [10]. Therefore, the sharper change of authenticity based on the proposed measure around threshold may lead to a sharper boundary between the surely authentic and unauthentic images, which is desirable for image authentication.

Fig. 8 shows the comparison results of different distance measures in terms of their discernable abilities. In Fig. 8(a), the last three columns are images maliciously tampered from the original portrait image *Lena*, by enlarging the eyes, modifying multiple objects in the image, and adding a small spot on the face. The others are images from acceptable manipulations including Gaussian noise introduction, auto contrast adjustment, sharpening, and lossy transmission (with error concealment). Fig. 8(b) shows results of image *Bike* with much stronger edges than image *Lena*. The last three columns of Fig. 8(b) are images tampered by deleting the saddle, modifying multiple objects (changing logo at the left top, modifying the display of the clock at right top, and deleting the

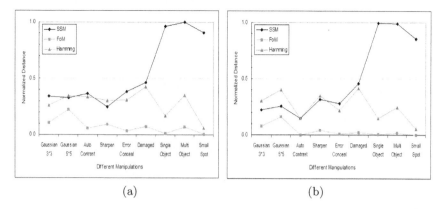

(a)   (b)

Fig. 8. Comparison of distinguish ability of different distance measures: only the proposed measure can successfully distinguish malicious manipulations from acceptable ones: (a) Results of image *Lena*; (b) Results of image *Bike*

saddle), and adding a small spot in the center of the right circle. Note that the *SSMs* were all below 0.5 for acceptable manipulations and all above 0.5 for maliciously attacked images. On the contrary, the Hamming and Figure of Merit (*FoM*) measures of maliciously attacked images were among the range of acceptable manipulations especially the measures of the attacked image in which there was a small local object changed (last column). The results show that the proposed *SSM* was able to distinguish the malicious manipulations from acceptable ones, i.e., identify lossy transmission as acceptable, and was sensitive to malicious manipulations. On the contrary, the Hamming and *FoM* measures were not sensitive to small localized object modification. The results indicate that the proposed *SSM* is more suitable for content-based image authentication than Hamming and *FoM* measures.

4.2   *SSM*-Based Error Resilient Image Authentication Scheme Evaluation

Robustness to Transmission Errors and other Acceptable Manipulations. The transmission errors in wireless networks were simulated based on the *Rayleigh* model [20] which is commonly used for wireless networks. Fig. 9(b) is an example of wavelet-based images damaged by transmission errors, and Fig. 9(c) is its error-concealed result. Fig. 9(d) is a DCT-based image damaged by transmission errors, and Fig. 9(e) is its error concealed result. The *SSM* values of image Fig. 9(c) and Fig. 9(e) are 0.134 and 0.250, i.e., the error-concealed images are both authentic.

With the set of images produced, an average peak signal-to-noise ratio (defined by *PSNR*) of 44.46 dB (Table 1) was obtained which is above the usually tolerated degradation level of 40 dB [23] and much better than the average 33.45dB in [13]. It is also better than the 42.47 dB obtained by the paper [23].

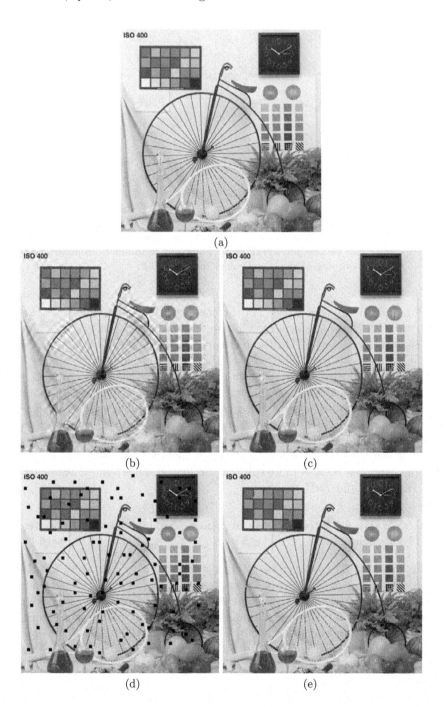

Fig. 9. Robustness against transmission errors: (a) original image (b) damaged image (wavelet based); (c) error concealed result of (b); (d) damaged image (DCT based); (e) error concealed result of (c)

Table 1. Comparison of objective quality decrease introduced by watermarking: *PSNR*(dB) of watermarked images

PSNR	Barbara	Bike	Airplane	Girl	Goldhill	Lena	Mandrill	Monarch	Pepper	Woman
Proposed	44.17	44.40	44.56	44.39	44.32	44.60	44.14	44.75	44.46	44.79
Ref. [13]	32.90	29.91	32.01	34.20	34.07	36.11	32.38	30.43	35.53	36.98
Ref. [23]	42.72	/	43.15	/	/	/	/	/	/	/

The quantization table used in these experiments is JPEG recommended quantization table of Q50. These results indicate the embedding procedure did not introduce visual artifacts in the images.

Table 2. Authentication performance improvement by error concealment: *PSNR* (dB) and *SSM* of damaged images and error-concealed images (BER1:10^{-4}; BER2:2×10^{-4})

Images		Actor	Bike	Chart	Flight	Fruits	Hotel	Lake	Lena	Pepper	Woman
Damaged	BER1	30.78	31.26	33.95	32.41	33.68	33.87	31.39	33.31	33.07	35.50
PSNR	BER2	25.87	25.76	28.51	26.05	27.81	26.71	25.68	30.34	27.74	30.72
Damaged	BER1	0.948	0.939	0.707	0.297	0.794	0.365	0.143	0.391	0.729	0.989
SSM	BER2	0.812	0.999	0.987	0.951	0.942	0.568	0.883	0.638	0.865	0.955
Recovered	BER1	38.03	41.76	41.11	41.03	39.90	42.40	38.54	40.21	41.25	42.96
PSNR	BER2	32.06	34.99	34.74	34.06	31.68	33.26	31.64	36.03	33.85	36.84
Recovered	BER1	0.158	0.134	0.141	0.035	0.204	0.067	0.057	0.345	0.089	0.329
SSM	BER2	0.220	0.099	0.446	0.072	0.406	0.045	0.280	0.059	0.182	0.015

Table 3. Robustness against acceptable image manipulations

Manipulations	Histogram Normalizing	Brightness Adjustment	Contrast Adjustment	JPEG Compression	JPEG2000 Compression
Parameter	Auto	-40	Auto	10:1	1bpp
SSM	0.159	0.159	0.262	0.017	0.057

Table 2 shows the evaluation results of the system robustness of the proposed error resilient image authentication scheme based on the proposed *SSM*. *PSNR* and *SSM* measures of the images damaged by transmission errors with different bit error rate (BER) 10^{-4} and 2×10^{-4}. The corresponding *PSNR* and *SSM* of the error-concealed images are also listed in this table. 60% of the damaged images at BER 10^{-4} and 100% at BER 2×10^{-4} in our experiments were verified as unauthentic. On the contrary, all error-concealed images were verified as authentic. These results indicate that our proposed scheme could obtain a good robustness to transmission errors. Note that on the contrary, the authentication scheme [23] was not robust to transmission errors. These results further confirm that it is effective and advisable for error concealment to be applied before image authentication. The reason that the authenticities of the recovered images were

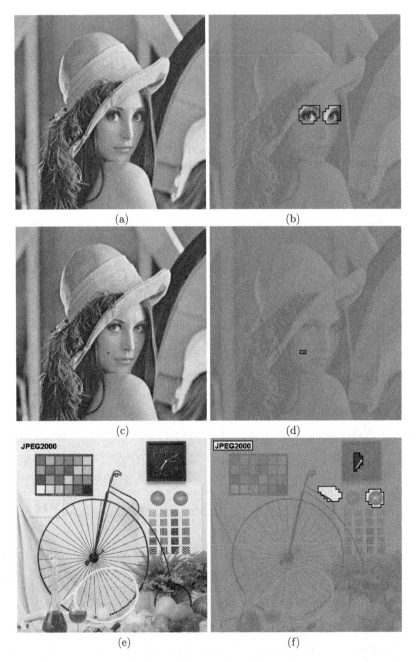

Fig. 10. Detected possible attack locations which are concentrated on objects in images: (a) noisy tampered image *Lena* (0.995); (b) attacked areas detected of (a); (c) *Lena* with small spot added (0.569); (d) attacked areas detected of (c); (e) attacked image *Bike* (logo modified, time modified, saddle deleted, and circle copied/pasted) (0.995); (f) attacked areas detected of (e)

better than those of the damaged images may be the image quality improvement by using error concealment on the damaged images [18], [20]. For example, the recovered image had much better objective qualities than the damaged images (evaluated by *PSNR*). This quality improvement made features of the error-concealed images closer to those of the original images than damaged images, so that the image authenticities (evaluated by *SSM*) of the error-concealed images were much larger than the damaged images.

Our scheme was also tested with other acceptable manipulations such as image contrast adjustment, histogram equalization, compression and noises addition. The results are shown in Table 3, with the parameter for each manipulation. The *SSM* values of these images were all less than 0.5, i.e., all these images can pass the authentication. These results validate that the proposed scheme is not only designed to be robust to transmission errors, but also robust to general acceptable manipulations.

Sensitivity to Malicious Content Tampering. An important aspect of our *SSM*-based authentication scheme is that it is sensitive to the malicious content tampering. For that reason, we tampered the previous watermarked *Bike* and *Lena* images and tested the ability of our system to detect and highlight the attacked areas. All the attacked images were detected and possible attacked areas were located. The attack location results are shown in Fig. 10.

These results indicate that the ability of our system to detect tampering is good even in the presence of multiple tampered areas (Fig. 10(e)), or noises (Fig. 10(a)), or very small area modified (Fig. 10(c)). Furthermore, the attack detection result of our scheme is friendly to users. If the image fails to pass the authentication, our scheme provides detected attacked areas which concentrate on objects. Further authentication decision can be made by the user with the aid of attack detection results.

5   Conclusions

A new feature distance measure based on statistical and spatial properties of the feature differences for content-based image authentication is proposed in this paper. The use of the typical patterns of feature differences by acceptable image manipulations and malicious content modifications did help improve system performance. Many acceptable manipulations which were detected as malicious modifications in the previous schemes were correctly classified into authentic images in the scheme based on *SSM*. The results also indicate that the statistical and spatial properties of the image feature are helpful and useful in distinguishing acceptable image manipulations from malicious content modifications. Moreover, the results would lead to a better understanding of the role of statistics and spatial properties of feature differences for detecting digital forgeries. The scheme was further evaluated under transmission errors.

The proposed feature distance measure is quite general and can be used in many other content-based authentication schemes provided that the features contain spatial information.

References

1. C. Y. Lin and S.F. Chang, "A Robust Image Authentication Method Distinguishing JPEG Compression from Malicious Manipulation", *IEEE Transaction on Circuits and Systems of Video Technology*, Vol.11, pp. 153-168, 2001.
2. E. Martinian, G. W. Wornell, and B Chen, "Authentication With Distortion Criteria", *IEEE Transaction on Information Theory*,Vol.51, No. 7, pp. 2523-2542, July 2005.
3. J. Dittmann, A. Steinmetz, and R. Steinmetz, "Content-based Digital Signature for Motion Pictures Authentication and Content-fragile Watermarking", *IEEE International Conference on Multimedia Computing and Systems*, Vol.2, pp.209-213, 1999.
4. B.B. Zhu, M.D. Swanson, and A.H. Tewfik, "When Seeing Isn't Believing: Multimedia Authentication Technologies", *IEEE Signal Processing Magazine*, Vol. 21, No. 2, pp.40-49, Mar 2004.
5. Y. Wang, J. Ostermann, and Y.Q. Zhang, "Video Processing and Communications", *Prentice Hall*, 2002.
6. M.P. Queluz, "Authentication of Digital Images and Video: Generic Models and a New Contribution", *Signal Processing: Image Communication*, Vol.16, pp. 461-475, January 2001.
7. E.C. Chang, M.S. Kankanhalli, X. Guan, Z.Y. Huang, and Y.H. Wu, "Robust Image Authentication Using Content-based Compression", *ACM Multimedia Systems Journal*, Vol. 9, No. 2, pp. 121-130, 2003.
8. Q. Sun and S.F. Chang, "Semi-fragile Image Authentication using Generic Wavelet Domain Features and ECC", *IEEE International Conference on Image Processing (ICIP)*, Rochester, USA, Sep. 2002.
9. S. Ye, Q. Sun, and E.C. Chang, "Error Resilient Content-based Image Authentication Over Wireless Channel", IEEE International Symposium on Circuits and Systems, Japan, 2005.
10. C. W. Wu, "On the Design of Content-Based Multimedia Authentication Systems", *IEEE Transactions on Multimedia*, Vol. 4, No. 3, pp.385-393, September 2002.
11. M. Schneider and S.F. Chang, "A Robust Content-based Digital Signature for Image Authentication", in *Proceedings of International Conference on Image Processing (ICIP)*, Vol.3, pp.227 - 230, 1996.
12. B. Li, E. Chang, and Y. Wu, "Discovery of a Perceptual Distance Function for Measuring Image Similarity", *ACM Multimedia Journal Special Issue on Content-based Image Retrieval*, Vol. 8, No. 6, pp.512-522, 2003.
13. Q. Sun, S. Ye, L.Q. Lin, and S.F. Chang, "A Crypto Signature Scheme for Image Authentication over Wireless Channel", *International Journal of Image and Graphics*, Vol. 5, No. 1, pp.1-14, 2005.
14. J. L. Cannons and P. Moulin, "Design and Statistical Analysis of a Hash-Aided Image Watermarking System", *IEEE Transaction on Image Processing*, Vol. 13, No. 10, October 2004, pp. 1393-1408.
15. R. Jain, R. Kasturi and B. G. Schunck, "Machine Vision", *McGraw Hill*, New York, 1995.

16. V. Erceg and K. Hari, "Channel Models for Fixed Wireless Applications", *IEEE 802.16 Broadband Wireless Access Working Group*, 2001.
17. P. Golle and N. Modadugu, "Authenticating Streamed Data in the Presence of Random Packet Loss", In *Proceedings of the Symposium on Network and Distributed Systems Security*, pp.13-22, 2001.
18. S. Ye, Q. Sun, and E.C. Chang, "Edge Directed Filter based Error Concealment for Wavelet-based Images", *IEEE International Conference on Image Processing*, Singapore, 2004.
19. W. Chou, "Classifying Image Pixels into Shaped, Smooth and Textured Points", *Pattern Recognition*, Vol. 32, No. 10, pp.1697-1706, 1999.
20. S. Ye, X. Lin and Q. Sun, "Content Based Error Detection and Concealment for Image Transmission over Wireless Channel", *IEEE International Symposium on Circuits and Systems (ISCAS)*, Thailand, May 2003.
21. M. Boliek (ed.), "JPEG 2000 Final Committee Draft", *ISO/IEC FCD*1.5444-1, Mar. 2000.
22. Y. Yu and S. T. Acton, "Speckle Reducing Anisotropic Diffusion", *IEEE Transaction on Image Processing*, Vol. 11, No. 11, Nov. 2002, pp.1260-1270.
23. A.H. Paquet, R.K. Ward, and I. Pitas, "Wavelet Packets-based Digital Watermarking for Image Verification and Authentication", *Signal Processing*, Special Issue on Security of Data Hiding Technologies, Vol. 83, No. 10, pp.2117-2132, October 2003.

LTSB Steganalysis Based on Quartic Equation

Xiangyang Luo[1,2], Chunfang Yang[1], Daoshun Wang[2], and Fenlin Liu[1]

[1] Zhengzhou Information Science and Technology Institute, Zhengzhou 450002, China
{xiangyangluo, chunfangyang}@126.com, liufenlin@vip.sina.com
[2] Department of Computer Science and Technology, Tsinghua University, Beijing
100084, China
daoshun@mail.tsinghua.edu.cn

Abstract. The LTSB (Least Two Significant Bit) planes steganalytic technique is discussed, and a detection method based on the Quartic Equation is presented. This method firstly constructs a finite-state machine including 16 kinds of state based on image pixel sample pairs, and then builds a quartic equation according to the states conversion relations, finally gains the estimated value by solving this equation. To enhance the precision of the estimate algorithm, an improved hypothesis is proposed, and a more robust quartic equation is constructed. Experiment results show that this approach can estimate the LTSB embedding ratio quite reliably.

1 Introduction

Steganography is one of the important research subjects in information security field. As a new art of covert communication, the goal of digital steganography is to convey messages secretly by concealing the very existence of messages under digital media files, such as images, audio, or video files. The study of steganography includes steganography and steganalysis. Among many steganography methods based on image, LSB (Least Significant Bit) steganography are now extremely widespread for its fine concealment, great capability of hidden message and easy realization. Similar to LSB steganography, LTSB (Least Two Significant Bit) steganography don't affect the vision effect of image, especially for the blue component of color image.

In LTSB steganography, the hidden messages are embedded into not only the LSB plane of the carrier, but also the hypo-least Significant Bit planes. Apparently, the capability of hidden message of LTSB steganography is twice as high as that of LSB steganography, and then it is very important to study LTSB steganalysis methods.

Presently, there are many LSB steganalysis methods, for example, χ^2-statistical analysis[1], RS steganalysis[2], RQP (the Raw Quick Pairs) steganalysis[3], the analysis method based on Laplace[4], SPA(Sample Pair Analysis) method[5] and the IQM steganalysis[6], where the SPA method detects LSB steganography via sample pair analysis and can estimate the LSB embedding ratio with high precision. Kinds of the improved RS and SPA methods are given in [7-10]. But LTSB steganalysis methods are scarce. For the LTSB embedding can modify not only LSBs,

Y.Q. Shi (Eds.): Transactions on DHMS II, LNCS 4499, pp. 68–90, 2007.

but also the hypo-least significant bits, although these LSB steganalysis detector performed well on the LSB steganography, they suffered from LTSB steganography, they aren't able to detect the LTSB steganography reliably.

Being enlightened by SPA method, this paper discusses the LTSB (Least Two Significant Bit) planes steganalysis technique, and presents a detection method based on the quartic equation. This method constructs a finite-state machine of 16 kinds of state based on image pixel sample pairs, then, builds a quartic equation via the states conversion relationships. Finally, the estimated value is gained by solving this equation. Experiments show that this approach can estimate the LTSB embedding ratio reliably.

The paper is organized as follows. In Section II, the construction of trace multisets and the finite-state machine are introduced. Then Section III describes how to establish a quartic equation about LTSB embedding ratio. The way to improve the accuracy of the estimated hidden message length is analyzed, and then a more robust quartic equation is presented in Section IV. Section V presents some experimental results with a test set of 500 continuous-tone images, and we conclude the paper in section VI. In order not to obscure the main contents, we give the necessary but lengthy proofs in the Appendices.

2   Trace Multisets and the Finite-State Machine

Assume that the digital image is represented by the succession of samples $s_1, s_2,$ $\cdots, s_N$ (the index represents the location of a sample in an image). A sample pair means a two-tuple$(s_i, s_j), 1 \leq i, j \leq N$. Let$P$, which is a set of sample pairs, be a multiset of the two-tuple(u, v), where u and v are the values of two samples drawn from a digitized image.

Denote by D_n the submultiset of P that consists of sample pairs of the form $(u, u + n)$ or$(u + n, u)$, i.e., the two values differ exactly by$n$, where n is a fixed integer,$0 \leq n \leq 2^b - 1$ and b is the number of bit to represent each sample value. In order to analyze the effects of LTSB embedding onD_n, it is useful to introduce some other submultisets of$P$. Since the embedding affects only the LTSB, the most significant $b - 2$ bits are utilized to choose these closed multisets. For each integer m, $0 \leq m \leq 2^{b-2} - 1$, denote by C_m the submultiset of P that consists of the sample pairs whose values differ by m in the first $(b-2)$ bits (i.e., by right shifting two bits and then measuring the difference).

Note that the multisets $D_n(0 \leq n \leq 2^b - 1)$ form a partition of P, and the multisets $C_m(0 \leq m \leq 2^{b-2} - 1)$ form another partition of P. D_n can be divided into multisets $D_{4m}, D_{4m+1}, D_{4m+2}$ and D_{4m+3}. It is clear that D_{4m} is contained in C_m. Indeed, if (u, v) is a pair in D_{4m}(i.e. $|u - v| = 4m$), then the LTSBs of u and v are equal. By right shifting two bits and taking the absolute difference, the value obtained is exactly $|u - v|/4 = m$, and hence, $(u, v) \in C_m$. It is not true, however, for D_{4m+1}, D_{4m+2} and D_{4m+3}.

When $n = 4m + 3$, if (u, v) is a pair in D_{4m+3}, then the pair can have one of the following forms:

$(4k, 4k-4m-3)$, $(4k-4m-3, 4k)$, $(4k+1, 4k-4m-2)$, $(4k-4m-2, 4k+1)$,

$(4k+2, 4k-4m-1)$, $(4k-4m-1, 4k+2)$, $(4k+3, 4k-4m)$, $(4k-4m, 4k+3)$

for some k. By right shifting two bits, these forms will become

$$(k, k-m-1), \quad (k-m-1, k), \quad (k, k-m-1), \quad (k-m-1, k),$$

$$(k, k-m-1), \quad (k-m-1, k), \quad (k, k-m) \text{ and } (k-m, k).$$

They consist of the samples whose values of first $(b-2)$ bits differ by $m+1$ or m. Hence, $(4k, 4k-4m-3), (4k-4m-3, 4k), (4k+1, 4k-4m-2), (4k-4m-2, 4k+1)$, $(4k+2, 4k-4m-1)$ and $(4k-4m-1, 4k+2)$ are contained in C_{m+1}, but $(4k+3, 4k-4m)$ and $(4k-4m, 4k+3)$ are contained in C_m. So D_{4m+3} is divided into two submultisets X_{4m+3} and Y_{4m+3}, where $X_{4m+3} = D_{4m+3} \cap C_{m+1}$ and $Y_{4m+3} = D_{4m+3} \cap C_m$, for $0 \leq m \leq 2^{b-2} - 2$, and $X_{2^b-1} = \Phi (\Phi$ denotes emptiset), $Y_{2^b-1} = D_{2^b-1}$.

Obviously, if the residual of the larger sample of the sample pair of D_{4m+3} divided by 4 is 0, 1 or 2, the sample pair is contained in X_{4m+3}, and if that of D_{4m+3} divided by 4 is 3, the sample pair is contained in Y_{4m+3}. Extensive experiments show that, for natural images, the probabilities that the residual of the larger sample of the sample pair of D_{4m+1} divided by 4 is 0, 1, 2 or 3 are equivalent. It means that, for any integer $m(0 \leq m \leq 2^{b-2} - 2)$,

$$E\{|X_{4m+3}|\} = 3E\{|Y_{4m+3}|\} \tag{1}$$

In order to construct the finite-state machine, X_{4m+3} is subdivided into three submultisets:

$$R_1 X_{4m+3}((4k+1, 4k-4m-2), (4k-4m-2, 4k+1)),$$
$$R_2 X_{4m+3}((4k, 4k-4m-3), (4k-4m-1, 4k+2)),$$
$$R_3 X_{4m+3}((4k-4m-3, 4k), (4k+2, 4k-4m-1)).$$

And Y_{4m+3} is regarded as submultiset $R_{11} Y_{4m+3}$.

For the same reason, submultisets $R_4 X_{4m+2}$, $R_5 X_{4m+2}, \ldots$, $R_{10} D_{4m}$, $R_{12} Y_{4m+2}, \ldots$, $R_{16} Y_{4m+1}$ and assumptions (2) and (3) can be obtained in followed Table 1.

$$E\{|X_{4m+2}|\} = E\{|Y_{4m+2}|\} \tag{2}$$

$$3E\{|X_{4m+1}|\} = E\{|Y_{4m+1}|\} \tag{3}$$

In this table, column 1 denotes the absolute difference of the pixel pairs and column 2 is the corresponding multiset. The multisets in column 3 are the partition of the multisets in column 2 and can be partitioned into the submultisets in column 4. Those in column 5 denote the forms of the pixel pairs in the submultisets in column 4. Last column gives the assumptions in two cases of different absolute differences. When $n = 4m$, where $0 \leq m \leq 2^{b-2} - 2$, the multiset D_{4m} is just divided into four submultisets.

Table 1. Partition of multisets and the assumptions

	multi-sets	multisets	submul-tisets	forms of pixel pairs	assumptions
$n = 4m + 3$ where $0 \leq m \leq 2^{b-2} - 2$	D_{4m+3}	X_{4m+3} $= D_{4m+3} \cap C_{m+1}$	$R_1 X_{4m+3}$	$(4k + 1, 4k - 4m - 2)$	$E\left\{\left|X_{4m+3}\right|\right\}$ $= 3E\left\{\left|Y_{4m+3}\right|\right\}$
				$(4k - 4m - 2, 4k + 1)$	
			$R_2 X_{4m+3}$	$(4k, 4k - 4m - 3)$	
				$(4k - 4m - 1, 4k + 2)$	
			$R_3 X_{4m+3}$	$(4k - 4m - 3, 4k)$	
				$(4k + 2, 4k - 4m - 1)$	
		Y_{4m+3} $= D_{4m+3} \cap C_m$	$R_{11} Y_{4m+3}$	$(4k + 3, 4k - 4m)$	
				$(4k - 4m, 4k + 3)$	
$n = 4m + 2$ where $0 \leq m \leq 2^{b-2} - 2$	D_{4m+2}	X_{4m+2} $= D_{4m+2} \cap C_{m+1}$ $X_{2^b - 2} = \Phi$	$R_4 X_{4m+2}$	$(4k, 4k - 4m - 2)$	$E\left\{\left|X_{4m+2}\right|\right\}$ $= E\left\{\left|Y_{4m+2}\right|\right\}$
				$(4k - 4m - 1, 4k + 1)$	
			$R_5 X_{4m+2}$	$(4k - 4m - 2, 4k)$	
				$(4k + 1, 4k - 4m - 1)$	
		Y_{4m+2} $= D_{4m+2} \cap C_m$ $Y_{2^b - 2} = D_{2^b - 2}$	$R_{12} Y_{4m+2}$	$(4k - 4m, 4k + 2)$	
				$(4k + 3, 4k - 4m + 1)$	
			$R_{13} Y_{4m+2}$	$(4k + 2, 4k - 4m)$	
				$(4k - 4m + 1, 4k + 3)$	
$n = 4m + 1$ where $0 \leq m \leq 2^{b-2} - 2$	D_{4m+1}	X_{4m+1} $= D_{4m+1} \cap C_{m+1}$ $X_{2^b - 3} = \Phi$	$R_6 X_{4m+1}$	$(4k, 4k - 4m - 1)$	$3E\left\{\left|X_{4m+1}\right|\right\}$ $= E\left\{\left|Y_{4m+1}\right|\right\}$
				$(4k - 4m - 1, 4k)$	
		Y_{4m+1} $= D_{4m+1} \cap C_m$ $Y_{2^b - 3} = D_{2^b - 3}$	$R_{14} Y_{4m+1}$	$(4k + 3, 4k - 4m + 2)$	
				$(4k - 4m, 4k + 1)$	
			$R_{15} Y_{4m+1}$	$(4k + 2, 4k - 4m + 1)$	
				$(4k - 4m + 1, 4k + 2)$	
			$R_{16} Y_{4m+1}$	$(4k + 1, 4k - 4m)$	
				$(4k - 4m + 2, 4k + 3)$	
$n = 4m$ where $0 \leq m \leq 2^{b-2} - 1$	D_{4m}		$R_7 D_{4m}$	$(4k, 4k - 4m)$	
				$(4k - 4m + 3, 4k + 3)$	
			$R_8 D_{4m}$	$(4k - 4m + 1, 4k + 1)$	
				$(4k + 2, 4k - 4m + 2)$	
			$R_9 D_{4m}$	$(4k + 1, 4k - 4m + 1)$	
				$(4k - 4m + 2, 4k + 2)$	
			$R_{10} D_{4m}$	$(4k - 4m, 4k)$	
				$(4k + 3, 4k - 4m + 3)$	

To summarize the assumption (1), (2) and (3), the following assumption is presented: for natural images,

$$E\left\{3\left|X_{4m+1}\right| + 2\left|X_{4m+2}\right| + \left|X_{4m+3}\right|\right\} = E\left\{\left|Y_{4m+1}\right| + 2\left|Y_{4m+2}\right| + 3\left|Y_{4m+3}\right|\right\} \tag{4}$$

In order to analyze the influence of LTSB embedding on sample pairs, let us consider all sixteen possible cases of LTSB flipping, labeled by sixteen so-called modification patterns π: $0000, 0001, \ldots, 1111$. From left to right, each 1 expresses that the hypo-least bit of the first sample, the least bit of the first sample, the least bit of the second sample or the hypo-least bit of the second sample of the sample pair has been reversed respectively, and 0 indicates that corresponding bit hasn't been reversed. For each m, $0 \le m \le 2^{b-2} - 1$, the submultiset C_m is partitioned into sixteen submultisets: $R_1 X_{4m-1}, R_2 X_{4m-1}, \ldots, R_{16} Y_{4m+1}$. It is clear that C_m is closed under the embedding, but this sixteen submultisets are not. Take an arbitrary sample pair (u, v) of $R_6 X_{4m-3}$. Then, $(u, v) = (4k, 4k - 4m + 3)$, or $(u, v) = (4k - 4m + 3, 4k)$. By modifying the sample pair (u, v) with the pattern 0011, the obtained sample pair is $(u', v') = (4k, 4k - 4m)$ or $(u', v') = (4k-4m+3, 4k+3)$. Thus all of the obtained sample pairs by modifying those in $R_6 X_{4m-3}$ with the pattern 0011 are included in $R_7 D_{4m}$.

Table 2. State-conversion table whose states are trace multisets of $C_m (m \ne 0)$

	R1	R2	R3	R4	R5	R6	R7	R8	R9	R10	R11	R12	R13	R14	R15	R16
R1	0000	0111	1101	0100	0001	0101	0110	1100	0011	1001	1010	1011	1110	1000	1111	0010
R2	0111	0000	1010	0011	0110	0010	0001	1011	0100	1110	1101	1100	1001	1111	1000	0101
R3	1101	1010	0000	1001	1100	1000	1011	0001	1110	0100	0111	0110	0011	0101	0010	1111
R4	0100	0011	1001	0000	0101	0001	0010	1000	0111	1101	1110	1111	1010	1100	1011	0110
R5	0001	0110	1100	0101	0000	0100	0111	1101	0010	1000	1011	1010	1111	1001	1110	0011
R6	0101	0010	1000	0001	0100	0000	0011	1001	0110	1100	1111	1110	1011	1101	1010	0111
R7	0110	0001	1011	0010	0111	0011	0000	1010	0101	1111	1100	1101	1000	1110	1001	0100
R8	1100	1011	0001	1000	1101	1001	1010	0000	1111	0101	0110	0111	0010	0100	0011	1110
R9	0011	0100	1110	0111	0010	0110	0101	1111	0000	1010	1001	1000	1101	1011	1100	0001
R10	1001	1110	0100	1101	1000	1100	1111	0101	1010	0000	0011	0010	0111	0001	0110	1011
R11	1010	1101	0111	1110	1011	1111	1100	0110	1001	0011	0000	0001	0100	0010	0101	1000
R12	1011	1100	0110	1111	1010	1110	1101	0111	1000	0010	0001	0000	0101	0011	0100	1001
R13	1110	1001	0011	1010	1111	1011	1000	0010	1101	0111	0100	0101	0000	0110	0001	1100
R14	1000	1111	0101	1100	1001	1101	1110	0100	1011	0001	0010	0011	0110	0000	0111	1010
R15	1111	1000	0010	1011	1110	1010	1001	0011	1100	0110	0101	0100	0001	0111	0000	1101
R16	0010	0101	1111	0110	0011	0111	0100	1110	0001	1011	1000	1001	1100	1010	1101	0000

A finite-state machine with sixteen states is built based on the sixteen trace submultisets of C_m. But because of the complexity of the finite-state machine, it is depicted via a state-conversion table (see Table 2). This table shows how the

Table 3. States-conversion table whose states are trace multisets of C_0

	$R_1 Y_1$	$R_2 Y_1$	$R_3 Y_1$	$R_4 Y_2$	$R_5 Y_2$	$R_6 Y_3$	$R_7 D_0$	$R_8 D_0$
$R_1 Y_1$	0000 1111	0111 1000	0010 1101	0100 1011	1110 0001	0101 1010	0110 1001	0011 1100
$R_2 Y_1$	0111 1000	0000 1111	0101 1010	0011 1100	1001 0110	0010 1101	0001 1110	0100 1011
$R_3 Y_1$	0010 1101	0101 1010	0000 1111	0110 1001	1011 0011	0111 1000	0100 1011	0001 1110
$R_4 Y_2$	0100 1011	0011 1100	0110 1001	0000 1111	1010 0101	0001 1110	0010 1101	0111 1000
$R_5 Y_2$	0001 1110	1001 0110	1100 0011	1010 0101	0000 1111	1011 0100	1000 0111	1101 0010
$R_6 Y_3$	0101 1010	0010 1101	0111 1000	0001 1110	1011 0100	0000 1111	0011 1100	0110 1001
$R_7 D_0$	0110 1001	0001 1110	0100 1011	0010 1101	1000 0111	0011 1100	0000 1111	0101 1010
$R_8 D_0$	0011 1100	0100 1011	0001 1110	0111 1000	1101 0010	0110 1001	0101 1010	0000 1111

sample pairs are driven from and to the sixteen trace submultisets by different LTSB modification patterns. The required modification patterns are filled into the blanks between the row states and arrange states. For facility, $R1$, $R2$,..., $R16$ replace the mentioned-above sixteen states.

The finite-state machine depicted in Table 2 does not apply to the multiset C_0. So need to model the behavior of C_0 under embedding separately. Multiset C_0 is closed under LTSB embedding and can be partitioned into R_1Y_1, R_2Y_1, R_3Y_1, R_4Y_2, R_5Y_2, R_6Y_3, R_7D_0 and R_8D_0. Then the transitions between them are illustrated in Table 3.

3 Construction of Estimation Equation

For each modification pattern $\pi \in \{0000, 0001, \cdots, 1111\}$ and any submultiset $Z \in P$, denote by $\rho(\pi, Z)$ the probability that the sample pairs of Z are modified with pattern π as a result of the embedding. Let p be the probability that a random bit of the LTSB planes of the image is modified. Therefore, the embedding rate is $4p$ bpp (bit per pixel). And replace $1 - p$ by q.

Assuming that the message bits of LTSB steganography are randomly embedded in the image, it can be gained that

$$\rho(0000, P) = q^4;$$
$$\rho(0001, P) = \rho(0010, P) = \rho(0100, P) = \rho(1000, P) = q^3p;$$
$$\rho(0011, P) = \rho(0110, P) = \rho(1100) = \rho(0101, P) = \rho(1010, P) = \rho(1001, P) = q^2p^2;$$
$$\rho(0111, P) = \rho(1110, P) = \rho(1101, P) = \rho(1011, P) = qp^3;$$
$$\rho(1111, P) = p^4$$

(5)

As a convention, Z or Z' denote each multiset, depending on whether the multiset is obtained from the original image or stego image after LTSB embedding. The same convention also applies to sample values such that (u, v) and (u', v') are the values of a sample pair before and after LTSB embedding. Consider that the message bits are randomly scattered in the LTSB below. So the conversion relations between the states depicted by Table 2 fetch the equation (6) (A proof of (6) is presented in Appendix A in order not to disrupt the presentation of our main ideas).

$$
\begin{pmatrix}
|R_1X'_{4m-1}| \\
|X'_{4m-1}| - |R_1X'_{4m-1}| \\
|X'_{4m-2}| \\
|X'_{4m-3}| \\
|D'_{4m}| \\
|Y'_{4m+3}| \\
|Y'_{4m+2}| \\
|Y'_{4m+1}| - |R_{15}Y'_{4m+1}| \\
|R_{15}Y'_{4m+1}|
\end{pmatrix}
= A \times
\begin{pmatrix}
|R_1X_{4m-1}| \\
|X_{4m-1}| - |R_1X_{4m-1}| \\
|X_{4m-2}| \\
|X_{4m-3}| \\
|D_{4m}| \\
|Y_{4m+3}| \\
|Y_{4m+2}| \\
|Y_{4m+1}| - |R_{15}Y_{4m+1}| \\
|R_{15}Y_{4m+1}|
\end{pmatrix}
$$

(6)

where

$$
A = \begin{pmatrix}
q^4 & qp^3 & q^3p & q^2p^2 & q^2p^2 & q^2p^2 & qp^3 & q^3p & p^4 \\
2qp^3 & q^4+q^2p^2 & 2q^2p^2 & 2q^3p & q^3p+qp^3 & 2qp^3 & 2q^2p^2 & p^4+q^2p^2 & 2q^3p \\
2q^3p & 2q^2p^2 & q^4+q^2p^2 & 2q^3p & q^3p+qp^3 & 2qp^3 & p^4+q^2p^2 & 2q^2p^2 & 2qp^3 \\
q^2p^2 & q^3p & q^3p & q^4 & q^2p^2 & p^4 & qp^3 & qp^3 & q^2p^2 \\
4q^2p^2 & 2q^3p+2qp^3 & 2q^3p+2qp^3 & 4q^2p^2 & 2q^2p^2+q^4+p^4 & 4q^2p^2 & 2q^3p+2qp^3 & 2q^3p+2qp^3 & 4q^2p^2 \\
q^2p^2 & qp^3 & qp^3 & p^4 & q^2p^2 & q^4 & q^3p & q^3p & q^2p^2 \\
2qp^3 & 2q^2p^2 & p^4+q^2p^2 & 2qp^3 & q^3p+qp^3 & 2q^3p & q^4+q^2p^2 & 2q^2p^2 & 2q^3p \\
2q^3p & p^4+q^2p^2 & 2q^2p^2 & 2qp^3 & q^3p+qp^3 & 2q^3p & 2q^2p^2 & q^4+q^2p^2 & 2qp^3 \\
p^4 & q^3p & qp^3 & q^2p^2 & q^2p^2 & q^2p^2 & q^3p & qp^3 & q^4
\end{pmatrix}
$$

Because of the fact that C_m can be divided into seven submultisets D_{4m}, X_{4m-1}, X_{4m-2}, X_{4m-3}, Y_{4m+1}, Y_{4m+2}, Y_{4m+3}, which can be known from the definitions of sixteen submultisets, the below equation can be outlined.

$$
|C_m| = |X_{4m-1}| + |X_{4m-2}| + |X_{4m-3}| + |D_{4m}| + |Y_{4m+1}| + |Y_{4m+2}| + |Y_{4m+3}| \quad (7)
$$

And since C_m will not vary after LTSB embedding, it follows that $C_m = C'_m$, viz.

$$
|C_m| = |X'_{4m-1}| + |X'_{4m-2}| + |X'_{4m-3}| + |D'_{4m}| + |Y'_{4m+1}| + |Y'_{4m+2}| + |Y'_{4m+3}| \quad (8)
$$

Solve the equation (6) and apply (7) and (8), then it can be obtained that (which are proved in Appendix B.)

$$
\begin{aligned}
(1-2p)^4 &(|Y_{4m+1}| + 2|Y_{4m+2}| + 3|Y_{4m+3}|) \\
&= 10p^4|C_m| + 4p^3(|X'_{4m-1}| + 2|X'_{4m-2}| + 3|X'_{4m-3}| - 3|Y'_{4m+3}| - 2|Y'_{4m+2}| \\
&\quad - |Y'_{4m+1}| - 5|C_m|) + p^2(-5|X'_{4m-1}| + |R_1X'_{4m-1}| - 9|X'_{4m-2}| - 12|X'_{4m-3}| \\
&\quad + 24|Y'_{4m+3}| + 15|Y'_{4m+2}| + |R_{15}Y'_{4m+1}| + 7|Y'_{4m+1}| + 13|C_m|) \\
&\quad + p(2|X'_{4m-1}| - |R_1X'_{4m-1}| + 3|X'_{4m-2}| + 3|X'_{4m-3}| - 15|Y'_{4m+3}| - 9|Y'_{4m+2}| \\
&\quad - |R_{15}Y'_{4m+1}| - 4|Y'_{4m+1}| - 3|C_m|) + |Y'_{4m+1}| + 2|Y'_{4m+2}| + 3|Y'_{4m+3}|
\end{aligned} \quad (9)
$$

and

$$
\begin{aligned}
(1-2p)^4 &(|X_{4m-1}| + 2|X_{4m-2}| + 3|X_{4m-3}|) \\
&= 10p^4|C_m| + 4p^3(-|X'_{4m-1}| - 2|X'_{4m-2}| - 3|X'_{4m-3}| + 3|Y'_{4m+3}| \\
&\quad + 2|Y'_{4m+2}| + |Y'_{4m+1}| - 5|C_m|) + p^2(7|X'_{4m-1}| + |R_1X'_{4m-1}| + 15|X'_{4m-2}| \\
&\quad + 24|X'_{4m-3}| - 12|Y'_{4m+3}| - 9|Y'_{4m+2}| + |R_{15}Y'_{4m+1}| - 5|Y'_{4m+1}| + 13|C_m|) \\
&\quad + p(-4|X'_{4m-1}| - |R_1X'_{4m-1}| - 9|X'_{4m-2}| - 15|X'_{4m-3}| + 3|Y'_{4m+3}| \\
&\quad + 3|Y'_{4m+2}| - |R_{15}Y'_{4m+1}| + 2|Y'_{4m+1}| - 3|C_m|) \\
&\quad + |X'_{4m-1}| + 2|X'_{4m-2}| + 3|X'_{4m-3}|
\end{aligned} \quad (10)
$$

Interchange m with $m+1$ in (10),

$$
\begin{aligned}
(1-2p)^4 &(|X_{4m+3}| + 2|X_{4m+2}| + 3|X_{4m+1}|) \\
&= 10p^4|C_{m+1}| + 4p^3(-|X'_{4m+3}| - 2|X'_{4m+2}| - 3|X'_{4m+1}| \\
&\quad + 3|Y'_{4m+7}| + 2|Y'_{4m+6}| + |Y'_{4m+5}| - 5|C_{m+1}|) \\
&\quad + p^2(7|X'_{4m+3}| + |R_1X'_{4m+3}| + 15|X'_{4m+2}| + 24|X'_{4m+1}| \\
&\quad - 12|Y'_{4m+7}| - 9|Y'_{4m+6}| + |R_{15}Y'_{4m+5}| - 5|Y'_{4m+5}| + 13|C_{m+1}|) \\
&\quad + p(-4|X'_{4m+3}| - |R_1X'_{4m+3}| - 9|X'_{4m+2}| - 15|X'_{4m+1}| \\
&\quad + 3|Y'_{4m+7}| + 3|Y'_{4m+6}| - |R_{15}Y'_{4m+5}| + 2|Y'_{4m+5}| - 3|C_{m+1}|) \\
&\quad + |X'_{4m+3}| + 2|X'_{4m+2}| + 3|X'_{4m+1}|
\end{aligned} \quad (11)
$$

Based on assumption (4), educe the following equation from (9)~(11)

$$
\begin{aligned}
&10p^4(|C_m| - |C_{m+1}|) + 4p^3(|X'_{4m-1}| + 2|X'_{4m-2}| + 3|X'_{4m-3}| + |X'_{4m+3}| \\
&+2|X'_{4m+2}| + 3|X'_{4m+1}| - 3|Y'_{4m+3}| - 2|Y'_{4m+2}| - |Y'_{4m+1}| - 3|Y'_{4m+7}| \\
&-2|Y'_{4m+6}| - |Y'_{4m+5}| + 5|C_{m+1}| - 5|C_m|) \\
&+p^2(7|Y'_{4m+1}| + |R_{15}Y'_{4m+1}| + 15|Y'_{4m+2}| + 24|Y'_{4m+3}| + 5|Y'_{4m+5}| \\
&+9|Y'_{4m+6}| + 12|Y'_{4m+7}| + |R_1 X'_{4m-1}| - 5|X'_{4m-1}| - 9|X'_{4m-2}| - 12|X'_{4m-3}| \\
&-7|X'_{4m+3}| - |R_1 X'_{4m+3}| - 15|X'_{4m+2}| - 24|X'_{4m+1}| \\
&-|R_{15}Y'_{4m+5}| + 13|C_m| - 13|C_{m+1}|) \\
&+p(2|X'_{4m-1}| + 3|X'_{4m-2}| + 3|X'_{4m-3}| + 4|X'_{4m+3}| + |R_1 X'_{4m+3}| + 9|X'_{4m+2}| \\
&+15|X'_{4m+1}| + |R_{15}Y'_{4m+5}| - 4|Y'_{4m+1}| - 9|Y'_{4m+2}| - 15|Y'_{4m+3}| - 2|Y'_{4m+5}| \\
&-3|Y'_{4m+6}| - 3|Y'_{4m+7}| - |R_1 X'_{4m-1}| - |R_{15}Y'_{4m+1}| + 3|C_{m+1}| - 3|C_m|) \\
&+|Y'_{4m+1}| + 2|Y'_{4m+2}| + 3|Y'_{4m+3}| - |X'_{4m+3}| - 2|X'_{4m+2}| - 3|X'_{4m+1}| \\
&= 0
\end{aligned}
$$

(12)

While $m = 0$, the equation (13) below can be obtained based on the conversion relations between states in the finite-state machine depicted in Table 3 (A proof of (13) is given in Appendix C).

$$
\begin{pmatrix}
|R_1 Y'_1| \\
|Y'_1| - |R_1 Y'_1| \\
|Y'_2| \\
|Y'_3| \\
|D'_0|
\end{pmatrix}
= B \times
\begin{pmatrix}
|R_1 Y_1| \\
|Y_1| - |R_1 Y_1| \\
|Y_2| \\
|Y_3| \\
|D_0|
\end{pmatrix}
$$

(13)

where

$$
B =
\begin{pmatrix}
q^4 + p^4 & q^3 p + q p^3 & q^3 p + q p^3 & 2q^2 p^2 & 2q^2 p^2 \\
2(q^3 p + q p^3) & q^4 + 2q^2 p^2 + p^4 & 4q^2 p^2 & 2(q^3 p + q p^3) & 2(q^3 p + q p^3) \\
2(q^3 p + q p^3) & 4q^2 p^2 & q^4 + 2q^2 p^2 + p^4 & 2(q^3 p + q p^3) & 2(q^3 p + q p^3) \\
2q^2 p^2 & q^3 p + q p^3 & q^3 p + q p^3 & q^4 + p^4 & 2q^2 p^2 \\
4q^2 p^2 & 2(q^3 p + q p^3) & 2(q^3 p + q p^3) & 4q^2 p^2 & q^4 + 2q^2 p^2 + p^4
\end{pmatrix}.
$$

The below equation can be educed from equation (13) (A proof of (14) is given in Appendix C).

$$
\begin{aligned}
&(1 - 2p)^4(|Y_1| + 2|Y_2| + 3|Y_3|) \\
&= 20p^4 |C_0| - 40p^3 |C_0| + p^2(2|Y'_1| + 2|R_1 Y'_1| + 6|Y'_2| + 12|Y'_3| + 26|C_0|) \\
&+p(-2|Y'_1| - 2|R_1 Y'_1| - 6|Y'_2| - 12|Y'_3| - 6|C_0|) + |Y'_1| + 2|Y'_2| + 3|Y'_3|
\end{aligned}
$$
(14)

Interchange m with 0 in (11),

$$
\begin{aligned}
&(1 - 2p)^4(|X_3| + 2|X_2| + 3|X_1|) \\
&= 10p^4 |C_1| + 4p^3(-|X'_3| - 2|X'_2| - 3|X'_1| + 3|Y'_7| + 2|Y'_6| + |Y'_5| - 5|C_1|) \\
&+p^2(7|X'_3| + |R_1 X'_3| + 15|X'_2| + 24|X'_1| - 12|Y'_7| \\
&-9|Y'_6| + |R_{15}Y'_5| - 5|Y'_5| + 13|C_1|) \\
&+p(-4|X'_3| - |R_1 X'_3| - 9|X'_2| - 15|X'_1| + 3|Y'_7| \\
&+3|Y'_6| - |R_{15}Y'_5| + 2|Y'_5| - 3|C_1|) + |X'_3| + 2|X'_2| + 3|X'_1|
\end{aligned}
$$

(15)

Finally, based on assumption (4), we can educe the following equation from (14) and (15)

$$
\begin{aligned}
&p^4(20\,|C_0| - 10\,|C_1|)\\
&+4p^3(|X_3'| + 2\,|X_2'| + 3\,|X_1'| - 3\,|Y_7'| - 2\,|Y_6'| - |Y_5'| + 5\,|C_1| - 10\,|C_0|)\\
&+p^2(2\,|Y_1'| + 2\,|R_1 Y_1'| + 6\,|Y_2'| + 12\,|Y_3'| + 5\,|Y_5'| + 9\,|Y_6'| + 12\,|Y_7'|\\
&\quad -7\,|X_3'| - |R_1 X_3'| - 15\,|X_2'| - 24\,|X_1'| - |R_{15} Y_5'| + 26\,|C_0| - 13\,|C_1|)\\
&+p(4\,|X_3'| + |R_1 X_3'| + 9\,|X_2'| + 15\,|X_1'| + |R_{15} Y_5'| - 2\,|Y_1'| - 2\,|R_1 Y_1'|\\
&\quad -6\,|Y_2'| - 12\,|Y_3'| - 3\,|Y_7'| - 3\,|Y_6'| - 2\,|Y_5'| - 6\,|C_0| + 3\,|C_1|)\\
&+|Y_1'| + 2\,|Y_2'| + 3\,|Y_3'| - |X_3'| - 2\,|X_2'| - 3\,|X_1'| = 0
\end{aligned}
\tag{16}
$$

All coefficients in quartic equation (12) and (16) can be counted from the image being examined for possible presence of LTSB embedding. Then, we can solve the equation (12) or (16) for p, $0 \le p \le 0.5$, which is a quarter of the estimated length of the embedded message.

4   Improving the Accuracy of Estimate

From Section 3, it can be seen that the proposed LTSB steganalytic technique hinges on assumption (4), and the estimated value $4\hat{p}$ primarily depends on the actual difference ε_m of assumption (4),

$$
\varepsilon_m = |Y_{4m+1}| + 2\,|Y_{4m+2}| + 3\,|Y_{4m+3}| - 3\,|X_{4m+1}| - 2\,|X_{4m+2}| - |X_{4m+3}| \tag{17}
$$

In order to improve the accuracy of the estimated algorithm, it is necessary to make $|\varepsilon_m|$ as small as possible.

However, a more robust estimate of hidden message length can be obtained by combining trace multisets across a range of m values in which $|\varepsilon_m|$ is small. For arbitrary $1 \le i \le j \le 2^{b-2} - 1$, use $\cup_{m=i}^{j} R_1 X_{4m-1}$, $\cup_{m=i}^{j} R_2 X_{4m-1}, \ldots,$ $\cup_{m=i}^{j} R_{16} Y_{4m+1}$ instead of $R_1 X_{4m-1}, R_2 X_{4m-1}, \ldots, R_{16} Y_{4m+1}$ in the finite-state machine depicted by Table 2, and extend C_m to $\cup_{m=i}^{j} C_m$. The multiset $\cup_{m=i}^{j} C_m$ is unbiased because the sixteen unions of trace multisets considered above are unbiased. Based on those, we can make the assumption

$$
\begin{aligned}
&E\left\{ 3\left|\cup_{m=i}^{j} X_{4m+1}\right| + 2\left|\cup_{m=i}^{j} X_{4m+2}\right| + \left|\cup_{m=i}^{j} X_{4m+3}\right| \right\}\\
&= E\left\{ \left|\cup_{m=i}^{j} Y_{4m+1}\right| + 2\left|\cup_{m=i}^{j} Y_{4m+2}\right| + 3\left|\cup_{m=i}^{j} Y_{4m+3}\right| \right\}
\end{aligned}
\tag{18}
$$

which is a more relaxed condition to satisfy than the hypothesis (4). In other words, $\left|\sum_{m=i}^{j} \varepsilon_m\right|$ tends to be significantly smaller than $|\varepsilon_m|$ for a fixed m, which is a determining factor of the accuracy of the proposed steganalytic approach. Note the equation (18) does not require the equation (4) to hold for all m. Instead, (18) only requires that for a sample pair $(u, v) \in P$ with $|u - v| \neq 4t$,

$i \leq t \leq j$, the probabilities that the sample pair is contained in $\cup_{m=i}^{j}(|X_{4m+1}| \cup |X_{4m+2}| \cup |X_{4m+3}|)$ or $\cup_{m=i}^{j}(|Y_{4m+1}| \cup |Y_{4m+2}| \cup |Y_{4m+3}|)$ satisfy the given relation by (18).

The trace multisets $\cup_{m=i}^{j} R_1 X_{4m-1}$, $\cup_{m=i}^{j} R_2 X_{4m-1}, \cdots$, $\cup_{m=i}^{j} R_{16} Y_{4m+1}$, where $1 \leq i \leq j \leq 2^{b-2} - 1$, have the same finite-state machine structure in Table 2 if the message is embedded randomly. Based on this finite-state machine structure and the assumption (18), the more robust equation to estimate the value of p is held.

$$
\begin{aligned}
&10p^4(|C_1| - |C_{j+1}|) \\
&+4p^3[2\sum_{m=1}^{j}(3|X'_{4m+1}| + 2|X'_{4m+2}| + |X'_{4m+3}| - 3|Y'_{4m+3}| - 2|Y'_{4m+2}| - |Y'_{4m+1}|) \\
&+|X'_3| - |X'_{4j+3}| + 2|X'_2| - 2|X'_{4j+2}| + 3|X'_1| - 3|X'_{4j+1}| \\
&+|Y'_5| - |Y'_{4j+5}| + 2|Y'_6| - 2|Y'_{4j+6}| + 3|Y'_7| - 3|Y'_{4j+7}| + 5|C_{j+1}| - 5|C_1|] \\
&+p^2[12\sum_{m=1}^{j}(|Y'_{4m+1}| + 2|Y'_{4m+2}| + 3|Y'_{4m+3}| - |X'_{4m+3}| - 2|X'_{4m+2}| - 3|X'_{4m+1}|) \\
&+5|Y'_{4j+5}| - 5|Y'_5| + 9|Y'_{4j+6}| - 9|Y'_6| + 12|Y'_{4j+7}| - 12|Y'_7| + 5|X'_{4j+3}| - 5|X'_3| \\
&+9|X'_{4j+2}| - 9|X'_2| + 12|X'_{4j+1}| - 12|X'_1| + |R_{15}Y'_5| - |R_{15}Y'_{4j+5}| + |R_1 X'_3| \\
&-|R_1 X'_{4j+3}| + 13|C_1| - 13|C_{j+1}|] \\
&+p[6\sum_{m=1}^{j}(3|X'_{4m+1}| + 2|X'_{4m+2}| + |X'_{4m+3}| - 3|Y'_{4m+3}| - 2|Y'_{4m+2}| - |Y'_{4m+1}|) \\
&+2|X'_3| - 2|X'_{4j+3}| + 3|X'_2| - 3|X'_{4j+2}| + 3|X'_1| - 3|X'_{4j+1}| + 2|Y'_5| - 2|Y'_{4j+5}| \\
&+3|Y'_6| - 3|Y'_{4j+6}| + 3|Y'_7| - 3|Y'_{4j+7}| + |R_1 X'_{4j+3}| - |R_1 X'_3| + |R_{15}Y'_{4j+5}| \\
&-|R_{15}Y'_5| + 3|C_{j+1}| - 3|C_1|] \\
&+\sum_{m=1}^{j}(|Y'_{4m+1}| + 2|Y'_{4m+2}| + 3|Y'_{4m+3}| - |X'_{4m+3}| - 2|X'_{4m+2}| - 3|X'_{4m+1}|) \\
&= 0
\end{aligned}
\tag{19}
$$

while $1 \leq j \leq 2^{b-2} - 2$.

Similarly, the equation as follows holds when $i = 0$.

$$
\begin{aligned}
&10p^4(2|C_0| - |C_{j+1}|) \\
&+4p^3[2\sum_{m=0}^{j}(3|X'_{4m+1}| + 2|X'_{4m+2}| + |X'_{4m+3}|) \\
&-2\sum_{m=1}^{j}(3|Y'_{4m+3}| + 2|Y'_{4m+2}| + |Y'_{4m+1}|) \\
&-|X'_{4j+3}| - 2|X'_{4j+2}| - 3|X'_{4j+1}| - |Y'_{4j+5}| \\
&-2|Y'_{4j+6}| - 3|Y'_{4j+7}| + 5|C_{j+1}| - 10|C_0|]] \\
&+p^2[12\sum_{m=1}^{j}(3|Y'_{4m+3}| + 2|Y'_{4m+2}| + |Y'_{4m+1}|) \\
&-12\sum_{m=0}^{j}(3|X'_{4m+1}| + 2|X'_{4m+2}| + |X'_{4m+3}|) \\
&+5|Y'_{4j+5}| + 9|Y'_{4j+6}| + 12|Y'_{4j+7}| + 5|X'_{4j+3}| \\
&+9|X'_{4j+2}| + 12|X'_{4j+1}| + 2|Y'_1| + 6|Y'_2| + 12|Y'_3| \\
&+2|R_1 Y'_1| - |R_{15}Y'_{4j+5}| - |R_1 X'_{4j+3}| + 26|C_0| - 13|C_{j+1}|] \\
&+p[6\sum_{m=0}^{j}(3|X'_{4m+1}| + 2|X'_{4m+2}| + |X'_{4m+3}|) \\
&-6\sum_{m=1}^{j}(3|Y'_{4m+3}| + 2|Y'_{4m+2}| + |Y'_{4m+1}|) \\
&-2|X'_{4j+3}| - 3|X'_{4j+2}| - 3|X'_{4j+1}| - 2|Y'_{4j+5}| \\
&-3|Y'_{4j+6}| - 3|Y'_{4j+7}| - 2|Y'_1| - 6|Y'_2| - 12|Y'_3| \\
&-2|R_1 Y'_1| + |R_{15}Y'_{4j+5}| + |R_1 X'_{4j+3}| - 6|C_0| + 3|C_{j+1}|] \\
&+\sum_{m=0}^{j}(|Y'_{4m+1}| + 2|Y'_{4m+2}| + 3|Y'_{4m+3}| - |X'_{4m+3}| - 2|X'_{4m+2}| - 3|X'_{4m+1}|) \\
&= 0
\end{aligned}
\tag{20}
$$

Solve this equation and choose the root p which is nearest to zero. Then multiply it by 4, the result $4p$ is the estimated length of the embedding message. A mass of experiments show that when $i = 0, j = 15$, and the sample pairs are composed of adjacent samplesthe estimated value is the most accurate.

5   Experimental Results

476 images in CBIB Image Database[11] and 24 standard images in Appendix D are collected and converted into 8-bit grayscale images. Then a new set of 500 cover images is created from these images. The proposed LTSB steganalytical technique is implemented and tested on this set of 500 continuous-tone images. The test set includes a wide range of natural images, from natural scenery to man-made objects like buildings and from panoramic views to close-up portraits. This makes the test results to be reported in this section indicative of the performance of the proposed steganalytical technique in reality. 22 groups of image are obtained by embedding 0 bpp, 0.05 bpp, 0.1 bpp, 0.2 bpp, ... , 1.9 bpp and 2.0 bpp message into the LTSBs of each image. To evaluate the performance of the new proposed detection method, these images are detected with QEM, LSM, SPA, hypo LSM and hypo SPA (all the pixel values are shifted 1 bit to the right, then applied SPA or LSM again) steganalysis methods.

First, the QEM method is applied to the set of 24 images in Appendix D and the estimated length of each image is given in Fig.1. The figure demonstrates that estimate values of the embedding ratio are close to the actual values, especially when the actual value is less than 170%. When the actual value of embedding ratio is too big, the estimate values become further away from the actual values, but the average estimate values still are reliable.

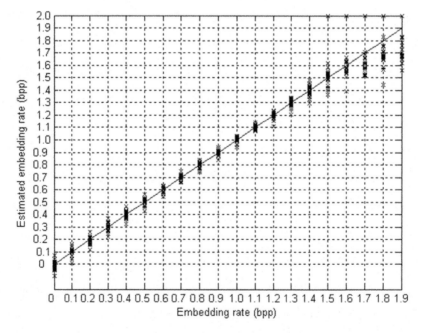

Fig. 1. Estimated embedding length of each image in Appendix D with different embedding rate gained with QEM

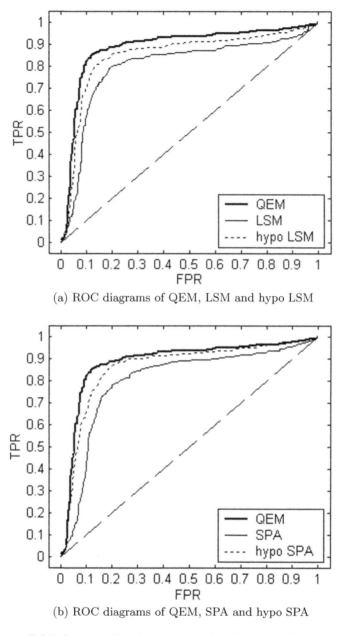

(a) ROC diagrams of QEM, LSM and hypo LSM

(b) ROC diagrams of QEM, SPA and hypo SPA

Fig. 2. ROC diagrams for 500 images with LTSB embedding at 0.05 bpp

Like the literatures [7] and [8], in order to compare the performance of QEM with those of other steganalysis methods, the Receiver Operating Characteristics (ROC) diagrams are given in Fig.2 and Fig.3 with LTSB embedding at 0.05 bpp and 0.1 bpp. Fig.2 and Fig.3 show that for LTSB embedding QEM works most

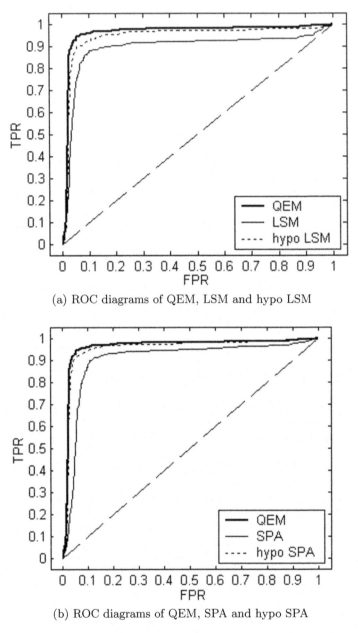

(a) ROC diagrams of QEM, LSM and hypo LSM

(b) ROC diagrams of QEM, SPA and hypo SPA

Fig. 3. ROC diagrams for 500 images with LTSB embedding at 0.1 bpp

effectively. Especially, the receivability of QEM becomes more apparent when LTSB embedding rate is lower than 0.1 bpp. In this paper, FPR means the false positive rate, TPR means the true positive rate.

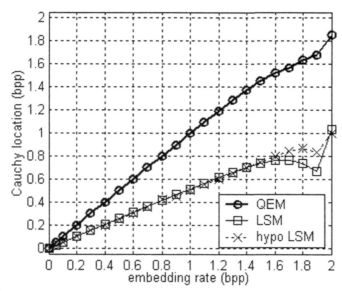

(a)The comparison among Cauchy locations of QEM, LSM and hypo LSM for different embedding rates

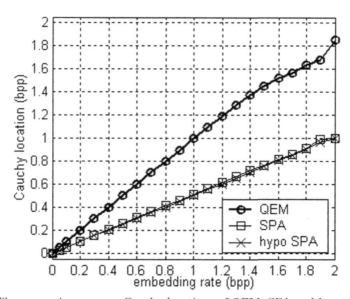

(b)The comparison among Cauchy locations of QEM, SPA and hypo SPA for different embedding rates

Fig. 4. Cauchy locations for 500 images with LTSB embedding

Since current length-estimating attacks face a high number of outliers, literature [12] showed that the errors for length estimations follow a Cauchy distribution better. So the accuracy of QEM is compared with those of LSM, hypo

LSM, SPA and hypo SPA on the location parameter of the Cauchy distribution. Namely, the location parameter of Cauchy distribution is used to instead of mean value. And the scale parameters of Cauchy distribution are given to tell the relative departure of estimated length of LTSB overwriting.

From Fig.4, it can be concluded that the proposed method outperforms LSM, hypo LSM, SPA and hypo SPA. The value of Cauchy location parameter with LSM, hypo LSM, SPA or hypo SPA is only about half of the actual embedding rate, but that of QEM is very close to the actual value. Fig.5 shows that the estimated embedding rate of QEM has considerable low departures of Cauchy location value.

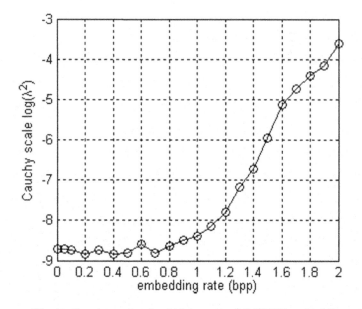

Fig. 5. Cauchy scales for 500 images with LTSB embedding

Because the new method is introduced to detect LTSB embedding, it does not act as well as LSM and SPA for LSB embedding. As can be seen from Fig.6, with the actual LSB embedding rate increasing from 0 to 1 bpp, the Cauchy location values is lower than half of the actual embedding rate about 0 bpp to 0.08 bpp. However, it still has higher reliability to detect LSB stego images by QEM, which can be seen from Fig.7.

When three groups of images are embedded into 0.1bpp message by LSB, hypo LSB and LTSB embedding, then QEM, LSM, hypo LSM, SPA and hypo LSM are applied to detect them. The ROC diagrams of them are plotted in Fig.8(a) and Fig.8(b). It can be found from Fig.8(a) and Fig.8(b) that QEM can detect those stego images with considerably high reliability, however LSM, hypo LSM,

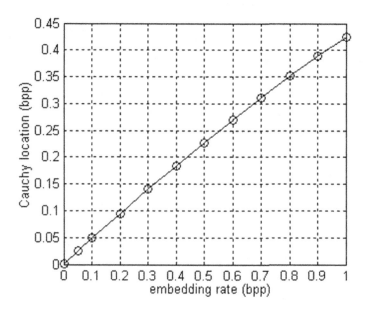

Fig. 6. Cauchy locations for 500 images with LSB embedding

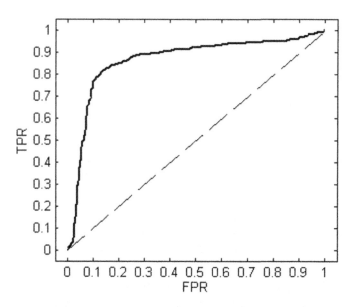

Fig. 7. ROC diagram of QEM for 500 images with LSB embedding at 0.1 bpp

SPA and hypo SPA do not perform very well. The results show that QEM not only can detect LTSB embedding precisely, but also can detect LSB embedding and hypo LSB embedding with rather high reliability.

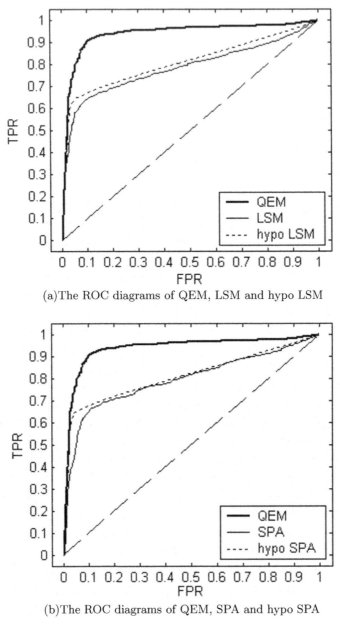

(a)The ROC diagrams of QEM, LSM and hypo LSM

(b)The ROC diagrams of QEM, SPA and hypo SPA

Fig. 8. ROC diagrams for three groups of images with LSB embedding, hypo LSB embedding and LTSB embedding at 0.1 bpp

6   Conclusions

This paper discusses the LTSB steganalytical technique, and presents a detection method based on quartic equation (QEM). This method constructs a finite-state machine based on image pixel sample pairs, and then builds a quartic equation via the states conversion relation. The estimated value is gained by solving this equation. In order to improve the accuracy of estimate algorithm, a more robust equation is built based on a more reliable assumption. It is concluded from extensive experiments that this approach can estimate the length of the LTSB embedded message with high precision. However, if message is only embedded into LSB plane, the assumption presented in this paper is not as desirable as those of SPA method, thus the estimate precision of the embedding ratio is not as high as that of the classic LSB steganalysis. But when the three kinds of stego images with LSB, hypo LSB and LTSB steganography are mixed, QEM have an obvious advantage in correct detection ratio than SPA and LSM steganalysis. How to improve the estimate precision of QEM for LSB steganography and how to identify the stego bit planes, unify the LSB, hypo LSB and LTSB steganalysis are our research directions in future.

Acknowledgments. The authors wish to thank the anonymous reviewers for their insightful and invaluable suggestions and comments. They would also like to thank Ms. Ping Wang for her programming assistance in this project. This work is supported by the Nation Natural Science Foundation of China (No. 60673082, 90304014), National High Technology Research and Development Program of China ("863" Program, No. 2006AA10Z409), and Henan Science Fund for Distinguished Young Scholar (No. 0412000200).

References

1. A. Westfeld. "Detecting low embedding rates", In: Proc. Information Hiding Workshop. Volume 2578 of Springer LNCS, (2002) 324–339.
2. J. Fridrich, M. Goljan, "Practical steganalysis of Digital Images – State of the Art", In: Proc. Security and Watermarking of Multimedia Contents IV. Volume 4675 of SPIE, (2002) 1-13.
3. J. Fridrich, R. Du, and L. Meng, "Steganalysis of LSB Encoding in Color Images," In: Proc. IEEE International Conference on Multimedia and Expo, New York, vol. 3, (2000) 1279–1282.
4. R. C.Gonzalez, P. Wintz, "Digital Image Processing", Addison-Wesley Publishing Company, Inc., 1997.
5. S. Dumitrescu, X. Wu, and Z. Wang, "Detection of LSB Steganography via Sample Pair Analysis", IEEE Transactions on Signal Processing, VOL.51, NO.7, (2003) 1995-2007.
6. I. Avcıbas, "Steganalysis Using Image Quality Metrics", IEEE Transactions on Image Processing, VOL. 12, NO. 2, (2003) 221-229.
7. Andrew D. Ker, "Improved Detection of LSB Steganography in Grayscale Images", In: Proc. The 6th Information Hiding Workshop.Volume 3200 of Springer LNCS, (2004) 97-115
8. Andrew D. Ker, "Quantitive evaluation of pairs and RS steganalysis", In: Proc. Security, Steganography, and Watermarking of Multimedia Contents VI. Volume 5306 of SPIE. 2004, 83-97.

9. P. Lu, X. Luo, and Q. Tang and et al. "An Improved Sample Pairs Method for Detection of LSB Embedding", In: Proc. The 6th Information Hiding Workshop.Volume 3200 of Springer LNCS(2004), pp.116-128.

10. X. Luo, B. Liu, and F. Liu. "Improved RS Method for Detection of LSB Steganography", In: Proc. the International Conference on Computational Science and Its Applications, Volume 3480 of Springer LNCS, (2005) 508-516.

11. CBIR Image Database. University ofWashington. 1997.
http://www.CS.washington.edu/research/imagedatabase/groundtruth/

12. R. Böhme. "Assessment of Steganalytic Methods Using Multiple Regression Models" In: Proc. 7th Information Hiding Workshop, Volume 3727 of Springer LNCS, (2005) 278-295.

Appendix A: Proof of Equations (6)

Based on the conversion relations among all sixteen states in the finite-state machine depicted by Table 2, we have

$$
\begin{pmatrix}
|R_1 X'_{4m-1}| \\
|R_2 X'_{4m-1}| \\
|R_3 X'_{4m-1}| \\
|R_4 X'_{4m-2}| \\
|R_5 X'_{4m-2}| \\
|R_6 X'_{4m-3}| \\
|R_7 D'_{4m}| \\
|R_8 D'_{4m}| \\
|R_9 D'_{4m}| \\
|R_{10} D'_{4m}| \\
|R_{11} Y'_{4m+3}| \\
|R_{12} Y'_{4m+2}| \\
|R_{13} Y'_{4m+2}| \\
|R_{14} Y'_{4m+2}| \\
|R_{15} Y'_{4m+2}| \\
|R_{16} Y'_{4m+2}|
\end{pmatrix}
= F \times
\begin{pmatrix}
|R_1 X_{4m-1}| \\
|R_2 X_{4m-1}| \\
|R_3 X_{4m-1}| \\
|R_4 X_{4m-2}| \\
|R_5 X_{4m-2}| \\
|R_6 X_{4m-3}| \\
|R_7 D_{4m}| \\
|R_8 D_{4m}| \\
|R_9 D_{4m}| \\
|R_{10} D_{4m}| \\
|R_{11} Y_{4m+3}| \\
|R_{12} Y_{4m+2}| \\
|R_{13} Y_{4m+2}| \\
|R_{14} Y_{4m+2}| \\
|R_{15} Y_{4m+2}| \\
|R_{16} Y_{4m+2}|
\end{pmatrix}
\tag{21}
$$

where

$$
F=
\begin{pmatrix}
q^4 & qp^3 & qp^3 & q^3p & q^3p & q^2p^2 & q^2p^2 & q^2p^2 & q^2p^2 & q^2p^2 & q^2p^2 & qp^3 & qp^3 & q^3p & p^4 & q^3p \\
qp^3 & q^4 & q^2p^2 & q^2p^2 & q^2p^2 & q^3p & q^3p & qp^3 & q^3p & qp^3 & qp^3 & q^2p^2 & q^2p^2 & p^4 & q^3p & q^2p^2 \\
qp^3 & q^2p^2 & q^4 & q^2p^2 & q^2p^2 & q^3p & qp^3 & q^3p & qp^3 & q^3p & qp^3 & q^2p^2 & q^2p^2 & q^2p^2 & q^3p & p^4 \\
q^3p & q^2p^2 & q^2p^2 & q^4 & q^2p^2 & q^3p & q^3p & q^3p & qp^3 & qp^3 & qp^3 & qp^3 & p^4 & q^2p^2 & q^2p^2 & q^2p^2 \\
q^3p & q^2p^2 & q^2p^2 & q^2p^2 & q^4 & q^3p & qp^3 & qp^3 & q^3p & q^3p & qp^3 & p^4 & q^2p^2 & q^2p^2 & qp^3 & q^2p^2 \\
q^2p^2 & q^3p & q^3p & q^3p & q^3p & q^4 & q^2p^2 & q^2p^2 & q^2p^2 & q^2p^2 & p^4 & q^3p & qp^3 & qp^3 & q^2p^2 & qp^3 \\
q^2p^2 & q^3p & qp^3 & q^3p & qp^3 & q^2p^2 & q^4 & q^2p^2 & q^2p^2 & p^4 & q^2p^2 & q^3p & qp^3 & qp^3 & q^2p^2 & q^3p \\
q^2p^2 & qp^3 & q^3p & q^3p & qp^3 & q^2p^2 & q^2p^2 & q^4 & p^4 & q^2p^2 & q^2p^2 & q^3p & qp^3 & qp^3 & q^2p^2 & q^3p \\
q^2p^2 & q^3p & qp^3 & qp^3 & q^3p & q^2p^2 & q^2p^2 & p^4 & q^4 & q^2p^2 & q^2p^2 & q^3p & qp^3 & qp^3 & q^2p^2 & q^3p \\
q^2p^2 & qp^3 & q^3p & qp^3 & q^3p & q^2p^2 & p^4 & q^2p^2 & q^2p^2 & q^4 & q^2p^2 & q^3p & qp^3 & qp^3 & q^2p^2 & q^3p \\
q^2p^2 & qp^3 & qp^3 & qp^3 & qp^3 & p^4 & q^2p^2 & q^2p^2 & q^2p^2 & q^2p^2 & q^4 & qp^3 & q^3p & q^3p & q^2p^2 & q^3p \\
qp^3 & q^2p^2 & q^2p^2 & p^4 & q^2p^2 & qp^3 & qp^3 & qp^3 & q^3p & q^3p & q^3p & q^4 & q^2p^2 & q^2p^2 & q^3p & q^2p^2 \\
qp^3 & q^2p^2 & q^2p^2 & q^2p^2 & p^4 & qp^3 & qp^3 & qp^3 & q^3p & q^3p & q^3p & q^2p^2 & q^4 & q^2p^2 & q^3p & q^2p^2 \\
q^3p & p^4 & q^2p^2 & q^2p^2 & q^2p^2 & qp^3 & qp^3 & qp^3 & qp^3 & q^3p & q^3p & q^2p^2 & q^2p^2 & q^4 & q^3p & q^2p^2 \\
p^4 & q^3p & q^3p & qp^3 & qp^3 & q^2p^2 & q^2p^2 & q^2p^2 & q^2p^2 & q^2p^2 & q^2p^2 & q^3p & q^3p & qp^3 & q^4 & qp^3 \\
q^3p & q^2p^2 & p^4 & q^2p^2 & q^2p^2 & qp^3 & q^3p & qp^3 & q^3p & qp^3 & q^3p & q^2p^2 & q^2p^2 & q^2p^2 & qp^3 & q^4
\end{pmatrix}
$$

It can be derived from the definitions of sixteen submultisets that

$$
\begin{cases}
|R_2X_{4m-1}| + |R_3X_{4m-1}| = |X_{4m-1}| - |R_1X_{4m-1}| \\
|R_2X'_{4m-1}| + |R_3X'_{4m-1}| = |X'_{4m-1}| - |R_1X'_{4m-1}| \\
|R_4X_{4m-2}| + |R_5X_{4m-2}| = |X_{4m-2}| \\
|R_4X'_{4m-2}| + |R_5X'_{4m-2}| = |X'_{4m-2}| \\
|R_6X_{4m-3}| = |X_{4m-3}| \\
|R_6X'_{4m-3}| = |X'_{4m-3}| \\
|R_7D_{4m}| + |R_8D_{4m}| + |R_9D_{4m}| + |R_{10}D_{4m}| = |D_{4m}| \\
|R_7D'_{4m}| + |R_8D'_{4m}| + |R_9D'_{4m}| + |R_{10}D'_{4m}| = |D'_{4m}| \\
|R_{11}Y_{4m+3}| = |Y_{4m+3}| \\
|R_{11}Y'_{4m+3}| = |Y'_{4m+3}| \\
|R_{12}Y_{4m+2}| + |R_{13}Y_{4m+2}| = |Y_{4m+2}| \\
|R_{12}Y'_{4m+2}| + |R_{13}Y'_{4m+2}| = |Y'_{4m+2}| \\
|R_{14}Y_{4m+1}| + |R_{16}Y_{4m+1}| = |Y_{4m+1}| - |R_{15}Y_{4m+1}| \\
|R_{14}Y'_{4m+1}| + |R_{16}Y'_{4m+1}| = |Y'_{4m+1}| - |R_{15}Y'_{4m+1}|
\end{cases}
\tag{22}
$$

To unite the components in (21) by the form of (22), then (6) is obtained.

Appendix B: Proof of Equations (9) and (10)

After uniting the components of equation (6) in the forms of

$$
|R_1X'_{4m-1}| + |X'_{4m-1}| - |R_1X'_{4m-1}| + 2|X'_{4m-2}| + 3|X'_{4m-3}|
$$
$$
-(|Y'_{4m+1}| - |R_{15}Y'_{4m+1}|) - |R_{15}Y'_{4m+1}| - 2|Y'_{4m+2}| - 3|Y'_{4m+3}|
$$

and

$$
|R_1X_{4m-1}| + |X_{4m-1}| - |R_1X_{4m-1}| + 2|X_{4m-2}| + 3|X_{4m-3}|
$$
$$
-(|Y_{4m+1}| - |R_{15}Y_{4m+1}|) - |R_{15}Y_{4m+1}| - 2|Y_{4m+2}| - 3|Y_{4m+3}|,
$$

then $|R_1X_{4m-1}|$, $|R_1X'_{4m-1}|$, $|R_{15}Y_{4m+1}|$ and $|R_{15}Y'_{4m+1}|$ are eliminated and followed equation holds:

$$
(1-2p)(|X_{4m-1}| + 2|X_{4m-2}| + 3|X_{4m-3}| - |Y_{4m+1}| - 2|Y_{4m+2}| - 3|Y_{4m+3}|)
$$
$$
= |X'_{4m-1}| + 2|X'_{4m-2}| + 3|X'_{4m-3}| - |Y'_{4m+1}| - 2|Y'_{4m+2}| - 3|Y'_{4m+3}|
\tag{23}
$$

After uniting the components of equation (6) in the forms of

$$
|R_1X'_{4m-1}| + (|X'_{4m-1}| - |R_1X'_{4m-1}|) + 2|X'_{4m-2}| + 3|X'_{4m-3}|
$$
$$
+(|Y'_{4m+1}| - |R_{15}Y'_{4m+1}|) + |R_{15}Y'_{4m+1}| + 2|Y'_{4m+2}| + 3|Y'_{4m+3}|
$$

and

$$
|R_1X_{4m-1}| + (|X_{4m-1}| - |R_1X_{4m-1}|) + |X_{4m-2}| + 3|X_{4m-3}|
$$
$$
+(|Y_{4m+1}| - |R_{15}Y_{4m+1}|) + |R_{15}Y_{4m+1}| + |Y_{4m+2}| + 3|Y_{4m+3}|,
$$

and applying the equation (7) it follows that

$$
(1-2p)^2(|X_{4m-1}| + |X_{4m-2}| + 3|X_{4m-3}| + |Y_{4m+1}| + |Y_{4m+2}| + 3|Y_{4m+3}|)
$$
$$
= |X'_{4m-1}| + |X'_{4m-2}| + 3|X'_{4m-3}| + |Y'_{4m+1}| + |Y'_{4m+2}| + 3|Y'_{4m+3}|
$$
$$
-(4p - 4p^2)|C_m|
\tag{24}
$$

Regard $|R_1 X_{4m-1}|$, $|X_{4m-1}|$, $|X_{4m-2}|$, $|X_{4m-3}|$, $|D_{4m}|$, $|Y_{4m+3}|$, $|Y_{4m+2}|$, $|Y_{4m+1}|$ and $|R_{15} Y_{4m+1}|$ as unknown quantities and others as known quantities, then (25) can be gained by using Matlab to solve the symbol equation (6).

$$
\begin{aligned}
&(1-2p)^4 \left(|X_{4m-2}| + |Y_{4m+2}|\right) \\
&= 2(p-p^2)\left|X'_{4m-1}\right| + 2(p^2-p)\left|R_1 X'_{4m-1}\right| + (2p^2-2p+1)\left|X'_{4m-2}\right| \\
&+ (2p^2-2p+1)\left|Y'_{4m+2}\right| + (2p^2-2p)\left|R_{15}Y'_{4m+1}\right| + (2p-2p^2)\left|Y'_{4m+1}\right| \\
&+ 2(2p^4 - 4p^3 + 3p^2 - p)\left|C_m\right|
\end{aligned} \tag{25}
$$

By multiplying by $(1-2p)^2$ both sides of (24) and adding the obtained equation to (25), we obtain

$$
\begin{aligned}
&(1-2p)^4(|X_{4m-1}| + 2|X_{4m-2}| + 3|X_{4m-3}| + |Y_{4m+1}| + 2|Y_{4m+2}| + 3|Y_{4m+3}|) \\
&= (20p^4 - 40p^3)|C_m| + 2p^2(\left|X'_{4m-1}\right| + \left|R_1 X'_{4m-1}\right| + 3\left|X'_{4m-2}\right| + 6\left|X'_{4m-3}\right| \\
&+ 6\left|Y'_{4m+3}\right| + 3\left|Y'_{4m+2}\right| + \left|R_{15}Y'_{4m+1}\right| + \left|Y'_{4m+1}\right| + 13|C_m|) \\
&- 2p(\left|X'_{4m-1}\right| + \left|R_1 X'_{4m-1}\right| + 3\left|X'_{4m-2}\right| + 6\left|X'_{4m-3}\right| \\
&+ 6\left|Y'_{4m+3}\right| + 3\left|Y'_{4m+2}\right| + \left|R_{15}Y'_{4m+1}\right| + \left|Y'_{4m+1}\right| + 3|C_m|) \\
&+ \left|X'_{4m-1}\right| + 2\left|X'_{4m-2}\right| + 3\left|X'_{4m-3}\right| \\
&+ \left|Y'_{4m+1}\right| + 2\left|Y'_{4m+2}\right| + 3\left|Y'_{4m+3}\right|
\end{aligned} \tag{26}
$$

And by multiplying by $(1-2p)^3$ both sides of (23), we obtain

$$
\begin{aligned}
&(1-2p)^4(|X_{4m-1}| + 2|X_{4m-2}| + 3|X_{4m-3}| - |Y_{4m+1}| - 2|Y_{4m+2}| - 3|Y_{4m+3}|) \\
&= 4p^3(-2\left|X'_{4m-1}\right| - 4\left|X'_{4m-2}\right| - 6\left|X'_{4m-3}\right| \\
&+ 6\left|Y'_{4m+3}\right| + 4\left|Y'_{4m+2}\right| + 2\left|Y'_{4m+1}\right|) \\
&+ p^2(12\left|X'_{4m-1}\right| + 24\left|X'_{4m-2}\right| + 36\left|X'_{4m-3}\right| \\
&- 36\left|Y'_{4m+3}\right| - 24\left|Y'_{4m+2}\right| - 12\left|Y'_{4m+1}\right|) \\
&+ p(-6\left|X'_{4m-1}\right| - 12\left|X'_{4m-2}\right| - 18\left|X'_{4m-3}\right| \\
&+ 18\left|Y'_{4m+3}\right| + 12\left|Y'_{4m+2}\right| + 6\left|Y'_{4m+1}\right|) \\
&+ \left|X'_{4m-1}\right| + 2\left|X'_{4m-2}\right| + 3\left|X'_{4m-3}\right| \\
&- \left|Y'_{4m+1}\right| - 2\left|Y'_{4m+2}\right| - 3\left|Y'_{4m+3}\right|
\end{aligned} \tag{27}
$$

Subtracting (27) from (26) leads to (7).

Adding (26) and (27) results in (after making the necessary cancellations and simplification) (10).

Appendix C: Proof of Equations (13) and (14)

Based on the conversion relations between state $R_1 Y_1$ and all eight states in the finite-state machine depicted by Table 3, we have

$$
\begin{pmatrix} |R_1 Y'_1| \\ |R_2 Y'_1| \\ |R_3 Y'_1| \\ |R_4 Y'_2| \\ |R_5 Y'_2| \\ |R_6 Y'_3| \\ |R_7 D'_0| \\ |R_8 D'_0| \end{pmatrix} = G \times \begin{pmatrix} |R_1 Y_1| \\ |R_2 Y_1| \\ |R_3 Y_1| \\ |R_4 Y_2| \\ |R_5 Y_2| \\ |R_6 Y_3| \\ |R_7 D_0| \\ |R_8 D_0| \end{pmatrix} \tag{28}
$$

where

$$G = \begin{pmatrix} q^4+p^4 & q^3p+qp^3 & q^3p+qp^3 & q^3p+qp^3 & q^3p+qp^3 & 2q^2p^2 & 2q^2p^2 & 2q^2p^2 \\ q^3p+qp^3 & q^4+p^4 & 2q^2p^2 & 2q^2p^2 & 2q^2p^2 & q^3p+qp^3 & q^3p+qp^3 & q^3p+qp^3 \\ q^3p+qp^3 & 2q^2p^2 & q^4+p^4 & 2q^2p^2 & 2q^2p^2 & q^3p+qp^3 & q^3p+qp^3 & q^3p+qp^3 \\ q^3p+qp^3 & 2q^2p^2 & 2q^2p^2 & q^4+p^4 & 2q^2p^2 & q^3p+qp^3 & q^3p+qp^3 & q^3p+qp^3 \\ q^3p+qp^3 & 2q^2p^2 & 2q^2p^2 & 2q^2p^2 & q^4+p^4 & q^3p+qp^3 & q^3p+qp^3 & q^3p+qp^3 \\ 2q^2p^2 & q^3p+qp^3 & q^3p+qp^3 & q^3p+qp^3 & q^3p+qp^3 & q^4+p^4 & 2q^2p^2 & 2q^2p^2 \\ 2q^2p^2 & q^3p+qp^3 & q^3p+qp^3 & q^3p+qp^3 & q^3p+qp^3 & 2q^2p^2 & q^4+p^4 & 2q^2p^2 \\ 2q^2p^2 & q^3p+qp^3 & q^3p+qp^3 & q^3p+qp^3 & q^3p+qp^3 & 2q^2p^2 & 2q^2p^2 & q^4+p^4 \end{pmatrix}$$

It can be derived from the definitions of eight submultisets that

$$\begin{cases} |R_2Y_1| + |R_3Y_1| = |Y_1| - |R_1Y_1| \\ |R_2Y_1'| + |R_3Y_1'| = |Y_1'| - |R_1Y_1'| \\ |R_4Y_2| + |R_5Y_2| = |Y_2| \\ |R_4Y_2'| + |R_5Y_2'| = |Y_2'| \\ |R_6Y_3| = |Y_3| \\ |R_6Y_3'| = |Y_3'| \\ |R_7D_0| + |R_8D_0| = |D_0| \\ |R_7D_0'| + |R_8D_0'| = |D_0'| \end{cases} \tag{29}$$

To unite the components in (28) by the form of (29), then (13) is obtained.

Because of the fact that C_0 can be divided into seven submultisets D_0, Y_1, Y_2, Y_3, followed equation can be had.

$$|C_0| = |D_0| + |Y_1| + |Y_2| + |Y_3| \tag{30}$$

And since C_0 will not vary after LTSB embedding, it follows that $C_0 = C_0'$, viz.

$$|C_0| = |D_0'| + |Y_1'| + |Y_2'| + |Y_3'| \tag{31}$$

After uniting the components of equation (13) in the forms of

$$|R_1Y_1| + |Y_1| - |R_1Y_1| + |Y_2| + 3|Y_3|$$

and

$$|R_1Y_1'| + |Y_1'| - |R_1Y_1'| + |Y_2'| + 3|Y_3'|,$$

and applying the equation (7), then $|R_1Y_1|$ and $|R_1Y_1'|$ will be eliminated and followed equation can be obtained.

$$(1-2p)^2(|Y_1| + |Y_2| + 3|Y_3|) = (|Y_1'| + |Y_2'| + 3|Y_3'|) + 4(p^2 - p)|C_0| \tag{32}$$

Regard $|R_1Y_1|$, $|Y_1|$, $|Y_2|$ and $|Y_3|$ as unknown quantities and others as known quantities, then (33) can be gained by using Matlab to solve the symbol equation (13).

$$\begin{aligned} (1-2p)^4\,|Y_2| &= (4p^4 - 8p^3)|C_0| + p^2(-2|Y_1'| + 2|R_1Y_1'| + 2|Y_2'| + 6|C_0|) \\ &\quad -p(-2|Y_1'| + 2|R_1Y_1'| + 2|Y_2'| + 2|C_0|) + |Y_2'| \end{aligned} \tag{33}$$

After doing the operation $(32)\times(1-2p)^2+(33)$ on equations (32) and (33), (14) is obtain.

Appendix D: 24 Typical Images

From 3D Mesh Data Hiding to 3D Shape Blind and Robust Watermarking: A Survey

Patrice Rondao Alface and Benoit Macq

Université catholique de Louvain,
Communications and Remote Sensing Lab.
Place du Levant 2, B-1348 Louvain-La-Neuve, Belgium
patrice.rondao@uclouvain.be, benoit.macq@uclouvain.be

Abstract. The need for secure communication of high value 3D virtual objects is becoming very important as a consequence of an increasing activity in simulation, entertainment, industrial design and cultural heritage. Secure communications of intangibles rely on cryptography and on watermarking of the transmitted objects to protect them against modifications (authentication watermarks) and redistributions (tracing forensic watermarks). While watermarking of image, audio and video is reaching maturity, 3D watermarking is still a technology in its infancy. Up to now, 3D watermarking has mainly focused on triangle meshes which are the most used digital representations of the shape of a 3D model. We show in this paper how recent signal processing techniques applied to meshes pave the way towards blind and robust watermarking of 3D shapes. We propose a survey of existing techniques and discuss their robustness, imperceptibility, capacity and security constraints.

1   Introduction

Over the last decennium, the digital rights management (DRM) problem of protecting data from theft and misuse has been addressed for many information types, including software code, digital images, videos and audio files. Demand for ways to similarly protect 3D graphical models is significantly growing. Scanned cultural heritage sculptures and artifacts, collaborative designed industrial models, graphical models used for online commerce or entertainment are examples of highly valuable contents that developers and owners are reluctant to distribute without control over piracy and reuse. This is the reason why there is an increasing need for watermarking of 3D models.

However, due to the very particular specificities of 3D objects, 3D watermarking is far from the maturity of watermarking algorithms dedicated to regularly sampled signals such as audio, image and video watermarking. 3D watermarking must cope with several challenging issues such as the non-euclidian nature of 3D meshes representing shapes as well as their usually irregular sampling which make difficult the extension of signal processing well-known tools. Other issues are related to the lack of adapted perceptive quality assessment tools, the variety of 3D attacks and the absence of consensus on 3D watermarking schemes

Y.Q. Shi (Eds.): Transactions on DHMS II, LNCS 4499, pp. 91–115, 2007.

requirements. It turns out that protecting a given 3D shape is very challenging knowing it can be represented with the same approximation error by many different meshes.

This survey first illustrates these specific problems and then presents a detailed overview of existing 3D mesh or 3D shape watermarking schemes. Section 2 introduces basic definitions and Sect. 3 presents an overview on 3D watermarking applications and 3D watermarking schemes requirements. Emphasis is put on the wide variety of 3D attacks and the challenges they pose for watermarking schemes. This section also focuses on watermark (and attack) imperceptibility assessing. Then Sect. 4 proposes a survey of existing watermarking schemes by highlighting their respective contributions and limitations. These schemes are classified by their embedding domain, distinguishing spatial, transform, attribute and compression domains. We present the intuition and main ideas of each referenced watermarking scheme and, where possible, we discuss their optimality in terms of robustness, capacity, imperceptibility and security. Section 5 concludes this survey by highlighting future research trends and remaining open issues.

2 Basic Definitions

3D virtual objects approximate a surface in the three-dimensional space. These objects can be represented by different structures such as *polygonal (or triangle) meshes*, *parametric surfaces* (such as Non-Uniform Rational B-Splines (NURBS), Bézier splines, Catmull-Rom splines...), *point-sampled surfaces*, *implicit surfaces*, *voxel-based representations* etc. However, the triangle is the basic geometric primitive for standard graphics rendering hardware and for many simulation algorithms. This fact partially explains why much of the work in the area of 3D watermarking deals with 3D triangle meshes. Although some schemes have been proposed to watermark NURBS (e.g. [36,31]) and point-sampled surfaces (e.g. [16]), we restrict this survey to 3D mesh watermarking schemes.

A 3D triangle mesh M can be seen as the embedding in the 3D space of geometric primitives: *vertices*, *edges* and *faces* (V, E, F). The set of these primitives are often referred to as the *connectivity* of the mesh. The embedding of vertices in the 3D space is named *geometry* and is represented by the set of the vertex coordinates (x, y, z). The vertices are also commonly referred to as *points* or *nodes*. Their number is noted n and ranges from 10^3 to 10^9.

Another important notion is the *topology* of a 3D mesh. This word is frequently used with different meanings in papers related to Computer Graphics and specifically to 3D watermarking. Indeed, topology can be referred to as:

- a synonym of connectivity [11].
- a description of the local geometric configuration of a face or vertex neighborhood [35].
- the mathematical study of the properties (genus, Euler characteristic, ...) of geometric solids or figures that are not changed by homeomorphisms [55].

These definitions are very different even though connectivity properties depend on the shape topology. In order to avoid confusions, we distinguish these different meanings by respectively naming them connectivity, local geometric configuration and shape topology [55].

3   3D Watermarking Applications and Requirements

This section presents the application context of 3D watermarking as well as the requirements of such applications. Readers not acquainted with watermarking vocabulary may find an excellent introduction in [17].

3.1   3D Watermarking Applications

3D watermarking applications may be classified following the general consensus on digital media watermarking [33]:

- Intellectual Property Rights (IPR) protection applications: This class of applications includes *copyright protection, fingerprinting, usage control* and *forensic.* For these applications, watermarking schemes are used to robustly convey information about content ownership and IPR.
- Content verification applications: The goal of the watermarking scheme in this case is to indicate whether the content has undergone any alteration and, in certain cases, to determine the type and location of such alteration. These applications are *authentication* and *integrity checking.*
- Data Hiding applications: In this class of applications, watermarks aim at conveying hidden information which is related or not to the content. Content-related information is mainly used for functionality enhancement purposes or for adding value to the content. Other kinds of hidden information are more related to steganography purposes.

The requirements of these three classes of application contexts are obviously very different. They are often described in terms of capacity, robustness, imperceptibility and security [17]. These watermarking scheme features are the topic of the following subsections.

3.2   Robustness and Attacks

Robustness concerns the ability of the embedded watermark to resist against a given class of usual or malicious manipulations of the content. These manipulations are often called *attacks.* General watermarking attacks can be classified in four categories following the analysis of Voloshynovskiy et al. [49]: removal attacks, geometrical attacks, cryptographic attacks, and protocol attacks. Such a classification has not been proposed yet for 3D watermarking attacks. In this survey, we follow the classification used by most authors of 3D watermarking papers.

- Similarity and affine transforms: *Rotation, uniform scaling* and *translation* (RST) transforms are mesh geometry modifications which are considered as common mesh manipulations. They are often referred to as *similarity transforms* and may be seen as the minimal requirement for a 3D watermarking scheme. *Non-uniform scaling, shear, projective distortions* are examples of more general *affine transforms* which are usually considered as intentional degradations of the mesh shape [4].
- Noising and de-noising: *Noising* attacks are usually performed by white gaussian noise addition on vertex coordinates. *De-noising* is usually performed by *Laplacian smoothing* [45]. This filter iteratively places each point in the barycenter of its point neighborhood. Other filters, described later in this paper, include curvature flow and transform domain smoothing.
- Connectivity attacks: Connectivity attacks modify the mesh adjacency information without modifying geometry. Among these attacks, *vertex reordering* is a manipulation which may desynchronize hidden data without any geometry or topology modification. Indeed, on the contrary of audio and image, the order of 3D mesh samples has no physical meaning. This attack has also been classified as a *distortion-less attack* in [18]. *Re-triangulation* is another connectivity attack which modifies triangles by edge flips.
- Sampling (or re-sampling) attacks: Sampling attacks are here referred to as attacks which modify the mesh geometry and connectivity but leaving its shape topology unchanged. These attacks are very common in practice and the most varied and challenging for a robust watermarking scheme [9]. In fact, a watermark aiming at protecting the 3D model shape should be robust to any modification of the sampling that preserves the shape visual perception. Sampling modifications include mesh *simplification* (removal of points and faces commonly used for a faster rendering [23]), mesh *refinement* (addition of points and faces usually by subdivision) and *remeshing* (local or global point density and connectivity changes)[2].
- Topological attacks: *Topological* attacks are complex attacks which may change the topological features of the mesh shape [55] (topological thus refers to shape topology). *Cropping* is the most well-known attack of this class. Most cropping attacks significantly degrade the shape but some of them preserve important parts of the shape that should also be protected (for example the head of the Michelangelo's David statue). Other possible attacks include imperceptible cuts and hole filling [55].
- Compression attacks: Since there is still no widely used mesh *compression* standard [1], the usual way to test the robustness of a watermarking scheme against compression algorithms consists in testing *point coordinates quantization*. This test also covers the truncation of vertex coordinates mantissas in effect of *format conversion* attacks.
- Geometrical deformations:These attacks are usually not handled in the literature with exception to [20] which proposes *bending* invariant signatures. Other complex geometrical transforms include mesh *editing*, mesh *morphing* and *local deformations* (for example addition of imperceptible small *bumps* [9]).

This list is of course not exhaustive but illustrates the relative wider variety of attacks a 3D watermarking scheme may undergo when compared with audio, image and video watermarking. It is obvious that neither watermarking nor attacks should affect the content so that the consecutive distortions become perceptible.

3.3 Imperceptibility

Assessing whether two shapes are differently perceived when rendered on a 2D screen is a difficult yet necessary task to evaluate imperceptibility. Most metrics used for benchmarking 3D watermarking schemes have been developed in the field of mesh simplification [23]. These are the *Hausdorff distance*, the *Root Mean Square Error* (RMSE) (a.k.a. *Vertex Signal-to-Noise Ratio* (VSNR)) and the *Geometric Laplacian Distortion Metric*. The Hausdorff distance is based on a point to surface distance [14], the RMSE and VSNR are based on mean point-to-point Euclidian distances [15] and the Geometric Laplacian proposed by Karni et al. [28] can be seen as the mean between point-to-point distances and a local smoothness evaluation. However, these metrics give poor estimations of the perception of the mesh shape since the human eye is much more sensitive to perturbations of a surface smoothness by random additive noise than to the smoothing of an already smooth surface yet producing the same metric error (Fig. 1).

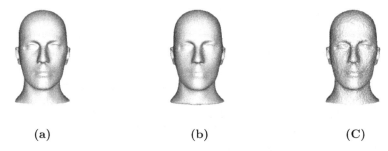

(a)   (b)   (C)

Fig. 1. Perception and usual 3D metrics. (a) the Stanford *head model*, (b) the same model after 430 iterations of Laplacian smoothing, (c) the same model after a noise addition of .17 percent. Comparing (a) with (b) and (a) with (c) with the RMSE metric leads to the same score of approximately .0001 while the perceived distortion is much more important for model (c).

As previously mentioned, many different meshes (with different connectivities and point densities) can represent the same continuous shape with very similar approximation errors (Fig. 2). Moreover, some lossy compression algorithms actually perform a complete remeshing of the shape as a preprocessing step [1]. Subsequently these different meshes are all representations of the same content. A robust watermark embedded to protect such content should therefore be retrieved on any remeshed version of this model producing the same perceived content through rendering.

Fig. 2. The same shape (*horse model*) represented by two different triangle meshes (data courtesy of Alliez and Gotsman [1]). The perception of both shapes are identical under usual rendering conditions. Point density variations and connectivity differences are smoothed and interpolated by usual shaders [21]. Both meshes therefore represent the same content.

The first attempts to model watermark or distortion perceptibility have focused on geometry curvature and geometry symmetries. For revealing the presence of a watermark, Benedens [8] has proposed to use the strategy of Zhou and Pang who present mean curvature diagrams and other curvature measures as metrics and visualization tools [59]. In 2003, Benedens has also shown that watermark embeddings which respect *reflective and axial symmetries* as well as *surface continuity* are less perceptible and more robust [9]. Surface discontinuity artifacts are generally smoothed by common interpolative shaders (Gouraud, Phong, ... [21]). These artifacts can be seen as high-frequency perturbations of the surface [28]. Moreover, some shape regions should be avoided for embedding such as sharp features (very common for CAD models) and curvature-constant regions (e.g. planar, spherical, cylindrical, ...).

Linking approximation errors with the human perception has first been explored for 3D watermarking by Corsini et al. [15], who propose a roughness-based metric to evaluate differences between original and watermarked versions of 3D meshes. This metric has been sucessfully validated through psycho-visual experiments inspired by ITU-T norms.

Similarly, Rondao Alface et al. [42] have proposed to compare rendered 2D images with a mutual information criterion (image-based metric). Psycho-visual experiments have also been run for 3D watermarking attacks such as noise addition, simplification and smoothing. Touch perception through haptic devices has also been explored to test the transparency of 3D watermarking algorithms by Prattichizzo et al. [40].

In conclusion, most watermarking schemes and attacks are cnstrained to be imperceptible. However, there is still a lack of standard tools enabling to assess such imperceptibility.

3.4 Capacity, Content and Security

Principles and intuition of 3D watermarking security do not differ much from the general watermarking case. Capacity however deserves some more observations. Indeed capacity is more difficult to estimate depending on the content aimed at by the application. For authentication and data hiding applications, the *mesh* representation is the content to protect. In these cases, capacity directly depends on the number of points or faces in the mesh. For the applications related to IPR protection, the content is the *shape* approximated by the mesh. The watermarking capacity related to the shape certainly depends on the curvature variations of the surface but the attempts to model it are at their very beginning (shape analysis based on information theory [38]).

3.5 3D Watermarking Schemes Requirements

As mentioned before, there is still no widely accepted consensus on 3D watermarking schemes requirements. Focusing on specificities related to 3D (requirements of general watermarking applications can be found in [17]), we present here a synthesis of the basic requirements proposed by authors of keystone 3D watermarking schemes [4,7,9,35,37,39,11,16,53]. These requirements depend on the target type of 3D model (CAD models, smooth digitalized models, non-manifold meshes ...) and on the application context. Alliez et al. have shown in [1] their review of recent advances of 3D mesh compression that there is still no compression algorithm that suits well for any kind of 3D mesh. These remarks also stand for 3D watermarking. Smooth models and meshes with sharp features or discontinuities show for example very different rate-distortion properties. The number of points of a mesh also influences the performances of algorithms which currently lack of scalability. Authors usually distinguish small meshes ($n < 10^4$), large meshes ($10^4 < n < 10^6$) and very large meshes ($n > 10^6$).

The context of application obviously determines the requirements of the watermarking scheme. Blind detection or retrieval should be preferred to informed detection whenever the availability of the original model implies a risk of misuse or theft [17]. Copyright protection thus demands blind detection (some side-information can however be tolerated). Integrity and authentication also require blind detection when the integrity of the original itself cannot be trusted. Moreover, using informed detection or retrieval necessitates the development of efficient database 3D shape retrieval algorithms to compare the original with the suspect mesh [8]. Blind detection (or retrieval) however involves many more challenges than informed detection and still leads to poor robustness results in practice.

Robustness requirements are the most difficult to determine. Integrity and authentication (as well as augmented contents) watermarking schemes should resist against RST transforms, lossless format conversion and vertex re-ordering and be fragile against all other attacks. Cayre et al. [13] however also propose cropping as an attack to which these schemes should be robust.

For copyright protection applications, robustness is required for all attacks preserving the visual perception of the shape. In practice, most papers proposing copyright protection 3D watermarking schemes only test RST transforms, vertex re-ordering, noise addition, compression, simplification, smoothing, cropping and subdivision. It is considered that the visual shape is the content to protect. Other kinds of properties of the mesh shape can also be important to protect such as touch perception (roughness and haptic textures properties) and functional imperceptibility. The latter concerns for example industrial CAD models which are virtually designed and then manufactured to be part of a complex system. Attacks and watermarks should not modify the design properties of such models.

In conclusion, each proposed watermarking scheme should carefully describe the target application and subsequent requirements.

4   3D Watermarking Schemes

In this survey, we describe most well-known and recent contributions to 3D watermarking. We classify them by the domain of embedding: spatial, transform, compression and attribute domains. This classification is further subdivided in function of the targeted application.

4.1   Spatial Domain

The 3D watermarking schemes which embed data in the spatial domain may be classified in two main categories : *Connectivity-driven* watermarking schemes and *Geometry-driven* watermarking schemes.

4.1.1   Connectivity-Driven Watermarking Schemes

We refer as *connectivity-driven* watermarking algorithms to those which make an explicit use of the mesh connectivity (some authors also refer to *topological features*, where topology must be understood as connectivity) to embed data in the spatial domain. These schemes are typically based on a public or secret traversal of all (or a subset of) the mesh triangles. The original model is usually not needed at the detection or decoding stage, they are therefore *blind* schemes. For each triangle satisfying an admissibility function, slight modifications are introduced in local invariants by changing the adjacent point positions. As a consequence, these schemes are sensitive to noise addition. However, well-designed embeddings may interestingly resist against some local connectivity modifications. Three main different strategies (a.k.a. *arrangements* [35], see Fig. 3) enable to re-synchronize the embedded data even after re-triangulation or cropping:

- Global arrangement: canonical traversal of all the connectivity graph.
- Local arrangement: canonical traversal of subsets of the connectivity graph.
- Subscript arrangement: explicit embedding of the localization of the information. This implies to hide both the data bit and its subscript as well.

If subscript arrangements need to embed more information than the local or global arrangements, they are usually more robust [11].

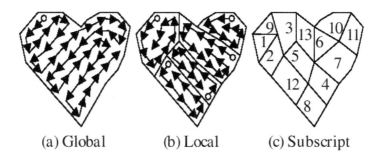

(a) Global   (b) Local   (c) Subscript

Fig. 3. Embedding strategies of connectivity-driven schemes: (a) global arrangement, (b) local arrangement, (c) indexed arrangement (data courtesy of Ohbuchi et al. [35])

Among this class of watermarking schemes, Ohbuchi et al. [35] have proposed four different watermarking algorithms in the first work published on 3D watermarking. These schemes are respectively named *Triangle Similarity Quadruple* (TSQ), *Tetrahedral Volume Ratio* (TVR), *Triangle Strip Peeling Sequence* (TSPS) and *Macro Density Pattern* (MDP). These schemes have inspired most connectivity-driven schemes developed so far. We classify these schemes by the application they target.

4.1.1.1   Data Hiding. Based on the fact that similar triangles may be defined by two quantities which are invariant to rotation, uniform scaling and translation (RST transforms), TSQ modifies ratios between triangle edge lengths or triangle height and basis lengths. A simple traversal of the mesh triangles is proposed to compute Macro-Embedding-Primitives (MEP). A MEP is defined by a marker M, a subscript S and two data values D_1 and D_2 (see Fig.4). Decoding is simply achieved by traversing each triangle of the mesh, identifying the MEPs thanks to the marker triangle. Then the subscript enables to re-arrange the encoded data D_1 and D_2. This scheme is invariant to RST transforms and to cropping thanks to the subscript arrangement. As security is not dealt with, this scheme can only be used for data hiding applications.

The invariant used by TVR is the ratio between an initial tetrahedron volume and the volume of tetrahedron given by an edge and the its two incident triangles. These ratios are slightly modified to embed the watermark and are invariant to *affine transforms*. Based on a local or global arrangement, TVR is a blind readable watermarking scheme. This scheme can only be applied on 2-manifold meshes (each edge has at most two incident faces). Benedens has extended this scheme to more general meshes without constraints of topology (*Affine Independent Embedding* AIE [8]). These schemes are however no more robust against cropping when compared to the TSQ scheme. These schemes can however hide f bits in a triangle mesh of f triangles which is much more than TSQ.

The third scheme, TSPS, encodes data in triangle strips given the orientation of the triangles. Based on a local arrangement, it presents the same robustness

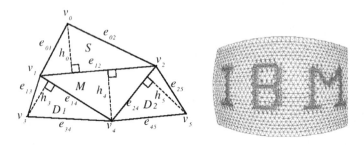

Fig. 4. On the left, Macro Embedding Primitive. For each MEP, the marker M is encoded by modifying the point coordinates of the triangle v_1, v_2, v_3 so that dimension-less ratios $l_{14}/l_{24}, h_0/l_{12}$ (l_{ij} stands for the length between vertices v_i and v_j) are set to specified values which will enable to retrieve marker triangles at the decoding stage. Then, the subscript is similarly encoded by modifying v_0 and subsequently $l_{02}/l_{01}, h_0/l_{12}$. Finally, data symbols D_1 and D_2 are encoded in $l_{13}/l_{34}, h_3/l_{14}$ and $l_{45}/l_{34}, h_5/l_{24}$ respectively. On the right, Macro Density Pattern example (data courtesy of Ohbuchi et al. [35]).

properties than the TSQ scheme. The capacity is difficult to estimate as the triangle strips generally do not transverse all the faces of the mesh. If it is not competitive with TSQ or TVR, this scheme is the basis of the best steganographic schemes presented in the sequel.

Finally, Ohbuchi's MDP is a visual watermarking method which embeds a meshed logo in the host model by changing the local density of points (see Fig.4). The logo is invisible with most common shading algorithms [21] but turns visible when the edges of the mesh are rendered. However, visible watermarking of 3D meshes has not many applications so far.

Focusing on the improvement of the mesh traversal simplicity and speed, O. Benedens has proposed another connectivity-driven scheme: the *Triangle Flood Algorithm* (TFA) [4]. This scheme uses connectivity and geometric information to generate a unique traversal of all the mesh triangles. Point positions are modified to embed the watermark by altering the height of the triangles and also to enable the regeneration of the traversal. This schemes exactly embeds $f - 1$ bits where f stands for the number of triangles.

4.1.1.2 Steganography. Cayre and Macq [11] have proposed a blind substitutive scheme which encodes a bit in a triangle strip starting from the triangle presenting the maximal area. This triangle strip is determined by the bits of a secret key, and determines the location of the encoded data in the 3D mesh. This scheme can be seen as an extension of TSPS with security properties which make it suitable for steganography purposes. It is indeed not possible to locate the embedded data without the knowledge of the secret key. For these reasons, this spatial substitutive scheme can also be considered as an extension of Quantized Index Modulation (QIM) schemes to 3D models.

Still considering steganography, Wang and Cheng [54] have improved the capacity of the precedent approach. First, they resolve the initial triangle for embedding by Principal Component Analysis (PCA). Next, an efficient triangular mesh traversal method is used to generate a sequence list of triangles, which will contain the hidden message. Finally, they embed three fixed bits per vertex for all vertices relying on three independent degrees of freedom. As a result, they exploit larger capacity in the 3D space. However, this capacity gain has been reached at some expense of the proved security features of the scheme of Cayre and Macq [11].

4.1.1.3 Authentication. Recently, Cayre et al. [13] have extended their previous scheme by using a global optimal traversal of the mesh and an indexed embedding. The authors specify the requirements of a 3D watermarking scheme for the authentication application context. They show their scheme withstands the attacks they consider in such context : RST transforms and cropping. For the cropping attack, the minimum watermark segment (MWS) is computed. They also propose a careful study of the capacity and security (in bits) of the embedding, the class of robustness and the probability of false alarm. The analysis of such features of a 3D watermarking scheme is difficult to perform for all other connectivity-driven watermarking schemes.

In conclusion, connectivity-driven algorithms are characterized by their relative fragility and their *blind decoding* capabilities. The embedded watermark does generally not resist against noise addition or global imperceptible re-triangulations (with exception to MDP). They are suitable for annotation and related applications only, with exception to more recent works which deal with the security issue [11,54] and [13]. These have been successfully designed respectively for steganographic and authentication purposes. Copyright or copy protection cannot be provided by this class of schemes as they do not resist against re-sampling.

4.1.2 Geometry-Driven Watermarking Schemes

This section presents the 3D watermarking schemes which embed data in the geometry. These schemes modify the point positions and/or the point (or face) normals. Point normals are estimations of the local continuous surface normal and are tied to the local shape of the mesh. On one hand, while surface sampling determines point positions, its influence on point normals is negligible if the point density is sufficient to accurately represent the surface. On the other hand, noise addition affects much more point normals and curvature estimations than point positions.

Notice some schemes need the orientation of face normals to be consistent and cannot be applied to non-orientable surfaces such as a Möbius strip. Point normals are usually estimated by a weighted sum of the adjacent faces normals or adjacent point positions. This means that a modification of the connectivity may affect the neighborhood of a point and have an impact on the point normal measure. However, attacks which modify point normals generally have a visual impact on the rendering of the mesh [21] and should therefore not be dealt with by a watermarking scheme.

4.1.2.1   Data Hiding. The *Vertex Flood Algorithm* (VFA) [5] embeds information in point positions. Designed for public watermarking, its high capacity is its
main feature. Given a point p in the mesh, all points are clustered in subsets (S_k)
accordingly with their distance to p. This point is the barycenter of a reference
triangle R whose edges are the closest to a predefined edge length ratio :

$$S_k = \{p_i \in V | k \le \frac{\|p_i - p\|}{W} < k+1\}, 0 \le k \le \lfloor \frac{d_{MAX}}{W} \rfloor \ , \tag{1}$$

where d_{MAX} is the maximal distance allowed from p, and W is the width of
each set. Each non-empty subset is subdivided in $m+2$ intervals in order to
encode m bits. The distance of each point in a subset is modified so that it is
placed on the middle of one of the $m+2$ intervals. The first and last intervals
are not used for encoding in order to prevent modifications of point distances
which would affect the other subsets. Decoding does not need the original mesh
and is simply achieved by reading point positions the subintervals in each subset
S_k. As the scheme of Harte et al., VFA only resists against RST transforms.
Compared to connectivity-driven watermarking schemes, this scheme can achieve
higher capacity, only limited by the point sampling rate and the point position
quantization precision.

4.1.2.2   Authentication. Yeo et al. [51] have developed an authentication algorithm by modifying point positions so that each mesh point verifies the following
equation:

$$K(I(p)) = W(L(p)) \ , \tag{2}$$

where $K(.)$ is the verification key, $I(p)$ is an index value depending on point coordinates, $W(.)$ is the watermark represented by a binary matrix and $L(p)$ gives
the location in the watermark matrix. $I(p)$ has been designed to be dependent
on the neighborhood of point p. This interesting feature allows the detection of
cropping attacks. Compared to connectivity-driven schemes also targeting authentication, the computational cost of this method is higher and the security
features have not been deeply analyzed.

4.1.2.3   Informed Copyright Protection. Informed or blind schemes dedicated
to copyright protection are often referred to as *robust watermarking schemes.*
The schemes should resist to all known manipulations and attacks which do not
produce a visible distortion on the 3D mesh. Schemes that resist to remeshing
and re-sampling are often referred as *3D shape watermarking schemes.*

The *Normal Bin Encoding* (NBE) scheme [4] embeds data in point normals.
Thanks to the curvature sampling properties pointed out before, this scheme
resists against simplifications of the mesh. Point normals are subdivided in *bins.*
Each bin is defined by a normal n_B named the *center normal* of the bin and
an angle ϕ_R called bin radius. If the angle between a point normal n_i is less
than ϕ_R then n_i belongs to such bin. Each bin encodes one bit of information by
using different features such as the mean of the bin normals, the bin mean angle
difference and the ratio of normals inside a threshold region determined by an

angle ϕ_K (with $\phi_K < \phi_R$). Point positions are modified so that the target value is assigned to the chosen bin feature. The decoding is simply achieved by computing the bins and their features but needs the original model for preprocessing purposes. This scheme has been improved later [8] and provides interesting imperceptibility and robustness features. The main drawback is the scalability of this technique which cannot efficiently handle meshes with more than 10^5 points.

Yu et al. [53] have proposed an informed robust scheme based on the histogram of the distances from the points of the surface to its center of gravity. This distance histogram is subdivided in bins and the points are iteratively displaced so that the mean or the variance of the histogram bin lies on the left or right of the bin middle to respectively encode a 0 or a 1. A scrambling of the vertices defined by a secret key is also proposed to secure the embedding of the watermark. The informed detection of the watermark necessitates the registration and resampling of the original and watermarked versions of the 3D model. The robustness features of this scheme cover noising and denoising attacks, cropping and re-sampling. Unlike NBE, this scheme has good scalability properties.

Focusing on imperceptibility criterions such as symmetry and continuity preservation, Benedens [7] has proposed a copyright protection watermarking scheme based on a *sculpting approach*. It uses Free Form Deformations (FFD) at distinct locations of the mesh (the so-called feature points) to embed a watermark. The basic steps performed by the embedding part of the algorithm consist in a first selection procedure of feature points and the displacement of these points along the surface normal (inwards or outwards depending on the watermark value) by a FFD. These two operations are ruled by secret keys. The detector is based on the assumption that random copies of the original model have features that are independently randomly distributed (i.e. independently randomly pointing inwards and outwards the surface following the same distribution). This algorithm presents very good imperceptibility and robustness results against noise addition, smoothing, cropping, affine transforms and a relatively good robustness against re-sampling. The latter strongly depends on the detector properties and registration optimality. Comparing the schemes of Yu et al. [53] and this scheme should be done by using the same fine registration and re-sampling process. It appears that the sculpting approach provides better imperceptibility results and comparable robustness features.

4.1.2.4 Blind Copyright Protection. Unlike informed robust watermarking schemes, these schemes cannot survive combined remeshing and cropping attacks so far. They also generally provide less robustness to geometric attacks. However, blind detection is a nice property that is usually required for a copyright protection application scenario. M. Wagner [50] has proposed a scheme which embeds data in the point normals of the mesh. These normal vectors are estimated by the *Laplacian operator* (a.k.a. *umbrella operator*) applied on the point neighborhood:

$$n_i = \frac{1}{d_{p_i}} \sum_{p_j \in N(p_i)} (p_j - p_i) \; , \tag{3}$$

where d_{p_i} is the number of point neighbors of p_i and $N(p_i)$ is the neighborhood of p_i. The watermark is a continuous function $f(p)$ defined on the unit sphere. Normal vectors n_i and the watermark function are converted in integers k_i and w_i respectively:

$$k_i = \lfloor \frac{c}{d} \|n_i\| \rfloor \tag{4}$$

$$w_i = \lfloor 2^b f \left(\frac{n_i}{\|n_i\|} \right) \rfloor , \tag{5}$$

where d is the mean length of these normal vectors, c is a parameter given by a secret key, and b is the number of bits needed to encode each w_i. The embedding proceeds by replacing b bits of k_i by those of w_i resulting in k_i'. Then the modified normals n_i' are re-computed by $n_i' = \frac{k_i' d}{c} \frac{n_i}{\|n_i\|}$. The watermarked coordinates of each point p_i' are obtained by solving the following system of $L + 1$ linear equations:

$$n_i' = \frac{1}{d_{p_i'}} \sum_{p_j' \in N(p_i')} (p_j' - p_i') . \tag{6}$$

However, it is not possible to build a surface from the sole point normal information and this linear equation system is indeed singular. In order to solve this issue, 20% of the points are not watermarked. The decoding of the watermark needs a modification of the parameter c because of the modification of the normal mean length d' : $c' = c \frac{d}{d'}$. In order to be robust to affine transforms, a non-Euclidian affine invariant norm [34] is used. The watermark can be either a visual logo on the unit sphere either a gaussian white noise. Scalability and computational cost of this scheme are a concern.

Harte et al. [25] have proposed another blind watermarking scheme to embed a watermark in the point positions. One bit is assigned to each point : 1 if the point is outside a bounding volume defined by its point neighborhood and 0 otherwise. This bounding volume may be either defined by a set of *bounding planes* or by an *bounding ellipsoid*. During embedding and decoding, points are ranked with respect to their distance to their neighborhood center. This algorithm is robust against RST transforms, noise addition and smoothing. Likewise the scheme of Wagner et al. [50], this scheme cannot withstand connectivity attacks such as remeshing or re-triangulation. However, this scheme presents a far better computational cost since embedding only needs one vertices traversal and limits computations for each point to the one-connected neighbors.

Cho et al. [18] have proposed a blind and robust extension of the scheme of Yu et al. [53]. This scheme presents the same robustness features with exception to cropping and any re-sampling attack that modifies the position of the center of gravity (e.g. unbalanced point density). They propose to send the position of this point to the detection side which is not realistic. Indeed, combined cropping and rotation or translation attacks can shift the relative positions of the model and the center of gravity conveyed as side-information. This scheme is limited to star-shaped models[1] but, considering robustness, outperforms the schemes of Harte et al. [25] and Wagner [50]. This scheme is however fragile against cropping.

Similarly, Zafeiriou et al. [57] have proposed to change the point coordinates into spherical coordinates with the center of gravity as origin. A Principal Component Analysis (PCA) is used to first align the mesh along its principal axes. Then two different embedding functions are used to modify geometric invariants. For angle *theta* and radius r, a continuous neighborhood patch is computed by a NURBS patch. A 0 is encoded if the center point radius is less than the mean radius of the neighborhood and a 1 is encoded otherwise. Similar to the scheme of Cho et al. [18], this scheme shows approximately the same advantages and limitations. This scheme is fragile against cropping and unbalanced re-sampling. Center of gravity shifts and PCA alignment perturbations [8] because of density sampling modifications are also a weakness which deserves further research.

More flexible than connectivity-driven algorithms, geometry-driven algorithms enable very different capacity-robustness trade-offs. If steganography and authentication seem better handled by the first ones, copyright protection techniques could be provided by geometry-driven schemes. However, there is still no blind and robust watermarking scheme able to resist against cropping and irregular point density re-samplings.

4.2   Transform Domain

This section is dedicated to watermarking schemes which embed information in a mesh transform domain. These transforms are extensions of regularly signal processing to 3D meshes: the mesh spectral decomposition, the wavelet transform and the spherical wavelet transform.

4.2.1   Spectral Decomposition

Spectral decomposition (a.k.a. pseudo-frequency decomposition or analysis) of 3D meshes corresponds to the extension of the well-known Discrete Fourier Transform (DFT) or Discrete Cosine Transform (DCT). This extension links the spectral analysis of matrices and of the spectral decomposition of signals defined on graphs [45,28]. The *pseudo-frequency analysis* of a 3D mesh is given by the projection of the geometry on the eigenvectors of the *Laplacian operator* defined on the mesh. The Laplacian is usually approximated by the umbrella operator $L = D - A$ where A is the adjacency matrix and D is a diagonal matrix with $D_{ii} = valence(p_i)$. Projecting the geometry canonical coordinates (X, Y, Z) leads to three real-valued spectra often noted (P, Q, R) [12]. Other Laplacian operator approximations have been successfully explored to design transforms which allow an optimal *energy compaction* in pseudo-low frequencies [58,3,56]. Since this transform is based on the eigen-decomposition of a n by n matrix, mesh connectivity partitioning must be used for meshes of more than 10^4 points to speed up the computation as well as avoiding numerical instabilities

---

[1] For each point of the surface, the segment linking this point to the center of gravity does not intersect the surface in any other point.

such as eigenvector order flipping [28,58]. Observing that partitioning induces artifacts on submesh boundaries, Wu et al. [56] have recently proposed radial basis functions (RBF) to compute the spectrum of 3D meshes with up to 10^6 points without the use of a partition algorithm. A better choice of coordinates than the canonical (X, Y, Z) to project on the spectral basis functions is still an open issue.

4.2.1.1 Informed Copyright Protection. The first scheme based on spectral decomposition has been proposed by Ohbuchi et al. in 2002 [37]. Their approach consists in extending spread-spectrum techniques to this transform. Well-balanced point seeds are interactively selected and initialize a connectivity-based front propagation which builds the partition. An additive watermark is embedded on low pseudo-frequency coefficients (P, Q, R) (the three spectra are embedded in the same way). The informed decoding retrieves the partition and the correspondence between the original connectivity and the watermarked geometry through registration, re-sampling and remeshing. This scheme presents robustness against RST transforms, noise addition, smoothing and cropping.

Benedens et al. [9] have improved the precedent scheme by embedding the watermark only in the transformed local normal component of the point coordinates instead of embedding (P, Q, R). They show this operation results in a better trade-off between imperceptibility and capacity. They show it improves the behavior of the decoder as well.

Cotting et al. [16] have extended the work of Ohbuchi et al. [37] to point-sampled surfaces. A neighborhood is still needed to compute the Laplacian eigenvectors and is provided by a k-nearest neighbors algorithm. A hierarchical clustering strategy is used to partition the surface. They also show that other point attributes such as color values can also be projected on the spectral basis functions and watermarked as well. The watermark is extracted through registration with the original and re-sampling. The re-sampling is based on the projection of new points on a polynomial approximation of the surface. Their algorithm presents robustness features very close to [37]. Furthermore, they show the watermark withstands repetitive embeddings of different watermarks.

Recently, Wu and Kobbelt [56] have proposed an approximation of the Laplacian eigenfunctions by RBF functions. These functions are centered on k (with $k << n$) seeds uniformly distributed on the mesh. A k by n matrix is then decomposed by Singular Value Decomposition (SVD). This scheme uses the embedding strategy of Ohbuchi et al. and presents the same robustness features while allowing real-time processing of large datasets without partitioning. However, when compared with schemes of Cotting et al. and Ohbuchi et al., this scheme presents less robustness because of the importance of selecting the same seeds for computing the RBF functions on the original model as well as on the suspected mesh at the detection side.

4.2.1.2 Blind Copyright Protection. Cayre et al. [12] have proposed a blind and substitutive watermarking scheme based on the flipping of spectral coefficient triplets (P, Q, R). An automatic partition of the connectivity is achieved as in [28].

Here, low pseudo-frequencies are avoided to improve the imperceptibility of the embedding. The watermark is on the contrary repeated on middle and high pseudo-frequencies. This scheme resists against RST transforms if the geometry is aligned on PCA axis. Robustness to smoothing and noise addition is comparable to the non-blind scheme of Ohbuchi et al. However, any modification of the connectivity implies a different partition and different laplacian matrices, which de-synchronises the watermarked data. When compared to geometry-driven blind robust schemes, the robustness to noise addition and smoothing is better using the spectral decomposition. The computational cost of the transform is however much higher.

Finally, the de-synchronization issue for blind spectral watermarking schemes has been explored by Rondao Alface et al. [41] who propose an automatic feature points detection to build a blind and robust partition. This partition is based on a geodesic Delaunnay triangulation leading to a feature base mesh. This base mesh is then remeshed by subdivision. Then each base triangle submesh is watermarked in the mesh spectral domain following the work of Cayre et al. [12]. The robustness to connectivity attacks of the latter approach is significantly improved by the feature points re-synchronization. However, the feature point robustness and the geodesic remeshing can still be improved to better resist against cropping and affine transforms attacks. Furthermore, some meshes may present too few feature points or generally non-uniformly distributed feature points which lead to a badly shaped base mesh. This results in a sub-optimal spectral decomposition and a low capacity.

In conclusion, spectral decomposition enables very good robustness results against watermarking attacks. Spectral watermarking schemes are promising but suffer from the weaknesses of the transform: eigen-decomposition of large matrices, choice of coordinates to project, and de-synchronization for blind watermarks by connectivity attacks. The first issue seems to find a convenient solution with RBF, the second and third have been recently explored but are still open issues.

4.2.2 Wavelet Transform

Wavelet decomposition and the multiresolution framework have also been extended to 3D triangle meshes. Lounsbery et al. [32] proposed a *lazy wavelet* transform. Each triangle of the mesh is quaternary subdivided and deformed to make it fit the surface to approximate. Wavelet coefficients are these local deformation vectors. Multiresolution analysis is computed with two analysis filters A^j and B^j for each resolution level j. Reconstruction is done with two synthesis filters P^j and Q^j which must satisfy:

$$\left[\frac{A^j}{B^j}\right] = \left[P^j | Q^j\right]^{-1} . \tag{7}$$

Let us call C^i the n^j by 3 matrix giving the coordinates of each point at the resolution level j. Then, we can write the following relations:

$$C^j = A^{j+1} C^{j+1} \tag{8}$$

$$D^j = B^{j+1} C^{j+1} \tag{9}$$

$$C^{j+1} = P^j C^j + Q^j D^j \ . \tag{10}$$

D^j represents the wavelet coefficients of the mesh, necessary to reconstruct C^{j+1} from C^j. Notice that from a theoretical point of view, columns of P^j are scaling functions and columns of Q^j are wavelet functions defined on the mesh topology. In practice, the lifting scheme is applied to build wavelet functions orthogonal to the scaling functions [32]. This transform can only be applied on semi-regular connectivity meshes because of the quaternary subdivision/simplification process. This drawback has been later solved by Valette et al. [47] which extend this scheme to arbitrary connectivity meshes.

4.2.2.1 Informed Copyright Protection. Kanai et al. [27] have proposed the first scheme embedding in the wavelet transform domain. Using the representation of Lounsbery [32], the watermark bits are embedded by modifying the least significant bits of the wavelet coefficients modulus. In order to minimize the visual impact of the watermark embedding, a selection of wavelet coefficients based on geometric thresholds is proposed. Watermark extraction is performed through the comparison of wavelet coefficients of the original and watermarked versions of the model.

Praun et al. [39] have proposed in 1999 an informed robust watermarking scheme which embeds a watermark in wavelet coefficients computed by *progressive meshes* [26] on which are defined RBFs which enable to locally deform the geometry. The embedding consists in the displacement of the points in normal or reverse-normal directions accordingly to the watermark value. The amplitude of this displacement is scaled by the RBF. The extraction of the watermark is performed through the registration and re-sampling of the original model with the watermarked model. This process actually modifies connectivity to make it fit with the original. This step significantly improves detection when compared with the scheme of Kanai et al. [27]. Moreover, this scheme is one of the most robust proposed so far. It resists against similarity, noise addition, connectivity, re-sampling, compression and cropping attacks. Benedens has shown in [9] the imperceptibility of the embedding can be improved by respecting model symmetries through the selection of symmetric features. Compared to other informed robust watermarking schemes, this scheme is the most robust to geometric attacks so far. Improving the registration process enables to also resist against large re-sampling attacks.

Yin et al. [52] have adopted the scheme in [24] to perform the multiresolution decomposition. Watermark information can be embedded into some spatial kernels of the low-frequency component of the shape. This strategy actually deals with the low-resolution representation in the geometry hierarchy which, however, does not not play the same role as the low-resolution components in the frequency domain. Unlike embedding a bit into the low-frequency domain, embedding a watermark bit into a vertex of the coarse mesh does not mean that the bit has been embedded globally into the low-frequency components of the whole mesh. For that reason the scheme is not robust against cropping operations. For other attacks, this scheme shares the same robustness properties as Praun et al. [39].

Spherical wavelets [43] have also been exploited for informed watermarking by Jin et al. [30]. Based on a spherical parameterization of the mesh starting from a canonical octahedron, the multiresolution analysis is close to the lazy wavelets and their corresponding watermarking schemes. Robustness and imperceptibility seem to be improved for genus-0 meshes (topologically equivalent to a sphere). Meshes approximating shapes of different topologies must first be converted in a genus-0 mesh trough hole fillings or cuts (see [55]) which leads to suboptimal results.

4.2.2.2 Blind Copyright Protection. Extending the scheme of Kanai et al., a blind watermarking algorithm has recently been proposed by Uccheddu et al. [46]. The main limitation of blind wavelet-based watermarking schemes is that they cannot withstand connectivity attacks. In the case of the scheme of Uccheddu et al., the input mesh is limited to have a prerequisite semi-regular subdivision connectivity. This limitation has been tackled by Valette et al. [47] by using lazy wavelets defined on arbitrary connectivities, but detection still cannot withstand connectivity attacks. These blind schemes present nearly the same robustness features as their Fourier-equivalent [12].

In conclusion, transform domain watermarking schemes show very good robustness properties for copyright and copy protection applications. Furthermore, wavelets enable the control of the local distortion caused by the embedding and low-frequency components of the spectral decomposition also present good properties when compared to the DCT and DFT for audio, image and video. However, schemes based on these transforms are characterized by a higher computation complexity than schemes embedding in the spatial domain. Scalability is therefore still a concern for very large meshes (with more than 10^6 points).

4.3 Compression Domain

As mentioned before, there is still no widely accepted 3D compression standard because of the lack of maturity of this field [1]. The watermarking schemes of this class are those which directly embed the watermark in the compressed data. Therefore, spectral- and wavelet-based schemes as well as some connectivity-driven schemes can also be classified (with some adaptations) in the compression domain category.

Denis et al. [19] have recently proposed a watermarking scheme based on the compression of 3D meshes through subdivision surface fitting. They have actually adapted the scheme of Ohbuchi et al. [37] to their specific transmission process. This scheme also highlights the difficulties inherent to a joint compression-watermarking strategy since it is less robust to noising and re-sampling attacks than the scheme of Ohbuchi et al. [37].

4.4 Attribute Domain

This category of schemes protects attribute data associated to the points or the faces of the mesh. These attributes can be texture, color, density, transparency etc. If scalar point and face attributes can be watermarked as geometry coordinates by transform-based schemes [37], textures need adapted schemes.

Garcia and Dugelay [22] embed the watermark in the texture of the model. Textures are images that are projected on the surface to enhance the visual content of the model itself. This process is called texture mapping. Embedding is performed by an image watermarking scheme. The decoding/detection phase consists in two steps: texture reconstruction from one ore several 2D views and detection of the watermark in the reconstructed texture. The original model is required to register 2D views and the watermarked model, hence this scheme is not blind. The correct estimation of the rendering conditions and projection parameters is the key to provide robustness to this scheme.

Obviously, compression and attribute domains have not yet received as much attention as spatial and transform domains. Attribute distortion imperceptibility has also not been deeply explored so far. However, these research areas raise more and more interest because of the success of analog research for images.

4.5   3D Embedding and 2D Retrieval

Interestingly, Bennour et al. [10] propose a very different approach to digital watermarking of 3D meshes. They embed the watermark in 3D silhouettes of the mesh and retrieve it in 2D rendered views of the model. Therefore, no 3D data is necessary at the decoding side, detecting unlicensed use of a model is directly processed on screen. This scheme resists against RST transforms and vertex reordering. Future work concerns robustness to simplification and the selection of key-views for embedding.

Table 1. Synthesis of the presented algorithms. Notations : data hiding (d.h.), steganography (steg.), authentication (auth.), informed copyright protection (i.c.p.), blind copyright protection (b.c.p.), spectral (s), wavelet (w),rotation-translation-uniform scaling (RST), vertex reordering (VR), laplacian smoothing (LS), noising (NO), cropping (CR), simplification (SI), re-sampling (RS), compression (CO), multiple watermarks (MW), not available (N-A), number of faces (f), number of points (n).

scheme	application	domain	robustness	capacity
[35,8,4]	d.h.	spatial	RST, VR	$\leq f/4$
[11,54]	steg.	spatial	RST, VR	$\approx 3n$
[51,5,13]	auth.	spatial	RST, VR, CR	$\leq n$
[39,27]	i.c.p.	transform (w)	RST, VR, NO, LS, CO, CR, SI, RS, MW	50
[53,7]	i.c.p.	spatial	RST, VR, NO, LS, CO, CR, SI, RS, MW	50
[4,50,8,25]	i.c.p.	spatial	RST, VR, NO, LS, CO, CR	32
[37,16,56]	i.c.p.	transform (s)	RST, VR, NO, LS, CO, CR, SI, RS, MW	32
[52,29,46]	b.c.p.	transform (w)	RST, VR, NO, LS, CO	N-A
[12]	b.c.p.	transform (s)	RST, NO, LS, CO	64
[41]	b.c.p.	transform (s)	RST, NO, LS, CO, SI	32
[18,57]	b.c.p.	spatial	RST, VR, NO, LS, CR, SI, RS	64

4.6 Synthesis

A synthesis of the presented watermarking schemes is given in Table 1. Schemes are classified by their application context, their embedding domain, their robustness and capacity. Since data hiding, authentication and steganography target the mesh elements, their capacity is given in terms of the number of faces or points. On the contrary, watermarking schemes for copyright protection target the shape and their capacity is usually set from 32 to 64 bits. A quantitative comparison of robust watermarking schemes is proposed in Table 2 for simplification and additive noise attacks. These attacks have been performed on the Stanford *Bunny* model which has been tested by almost all authors cited in this survey. The source of these robustness results are the corresponding and aforementioned referenced publications.

Table 2. Quantitative comparison of robust watermarking schemes for additive noise and simplification attacks on the Stanford *Bunny* model. Transform (s) and (w) respectively stand for spectral decomposition and wavelet transform. Noise addition results refer to the noise amplitude expressed in percentage of the bounding box diagonal (high values correspond to a good robustness). Simplification results are given as the ratio of the number of points after and before the simplification attack (low values correspond to a good robustness). It is however difficult to know which simplification algorithm has been used by the authors of most schemes. These comparative results should therefore be considered as a rough estimation.

scheme	detection/decoding	domain	noise	simplification
[39]	informed	transform (w)	.70%	.125
[30]	informed	transform (w)	.06%	.125
[16]	informed	transform (s)	.10%	.5
[18]	blind	spatial	.10%	.5
[11]	blind	transform (s)	.44%	-
[46]	blind	transform (w)	.17%	-
[47]	blind	transform (w)	.45%	-

5 Conclusions

This survey has presented the evolution of watermarking technology from mesh protection to shape protection. This evolution copes with a large set of open and challenging issues.

Hiding data in mesh elements such as triangles or point coordinates in order to resist to RST transforms and vertex re-ordering has been solved in many ways even though there is still work left for security, computational cost and capacity optimization.

Protecting shapes for forensic applications has been deeply explored. A wide set of original techniques have been proposed based on signal processing extensions to irregularly sampled and manifold data. Their robustness tends to be satisfactory and now directly depends on the quality of the resynchronization with the original mesh.

However, there is still a need for a more careful analysis on how to modulate the watermark strength accordingly to the local perceived distortion. Assessing the watermarking capacity of a shape according to its curvature information (independently of its mesh representation) is another issue that deserves more research.

Beside these new challenges for informed watermarking schemes, it turns out that blind detection or retrieval is more suitable for copyright protection applications. In this case, although the considerable efforts spent on extending informed techniques to blind detection, there is still no algorithm able to withstand combined cropping and re-sampling attacks.

Finally, there is still no benchmarking platform for 3D watermarking schemes. They would however certainly be desirable for comparing schemes performances and improving their design.

Acknowledgments. The authors thank François Cayre, Massimiliano Corsini, Horace Ip and Wolfgang Funk for helpful discussions. We are also grateful to the anonymous reviewers who have helped to improve the quality of this paper. Patrice Rondao Alface is funded by a Belgian F.R.I.A. grant from the Communauté française de Belgique.

References

1. Alliez, P., Gotsman, C.: Recent advances in compression of 3D meshes. Advances in Multiresolution for Geometric Modelling. Dogson, N.A., Floater, M.S., Sabin, M.A. (Springer-Verlag eds.) ISBN 3-540-21462-3 (2002) 3–26.
2. Alliez, P., Ucelli, G., Gotsman, C., Attene, M.: Recent Advances in Remeshing of Surfaces. Shape Analysis and Structuring, De Floriani, L., Spagnuolo M. (eds.), Springer-Verlag, (2006), *to appear*.
3. Ben-Chen, M., Gotsman, C.: On the optimality of spectral compression of mesh data. ACM Transactions on Graphics **24(1)** (2005) 60-80.
4. Benedens, O.: Geometry-based watermarking of 3D models. IEEE Computer Graphics and Applications **Vol. 19 No. 1** (1999) 46–55.
5. Benedens, O.: Two high capacity methods for embedding public watermarks into 3D polygonal models. In Proceedings of ACM Multimedia (1999) 95–99.
6. Benedens, O., Bush, C.: Towards Blind Detection of Robust Watermarks. EUROGRAPHICS00, Gross, M., Hopgood, F.R.A. eds. **19(3)** (2000) 199–209.
7. Benedens, O.: Robust Watermarking and Affine Registration of 3D Meshes. In Proc. of 5th International Workshop on Information Hiding, NoordWijkerhout, Netherlands, October 7-9 (2002) 177-195.
8. Benedens, O.: 3D Watermarking Algorithms in Context of OpenSG Plus. Technical Report 02i002-figd (2002).
9. Benedens, O., Dittman, J., Petitcolas, F.A.P.: 3D Watermarking Design Evaluation. Security and Watermarking of Multimedia Contents V, Delp, E.J., Wong, P.W., Eds., Proc. of SPIE-IS&T Electronic Imaging, SPIE **Vol. 5020** (2003) 337–348.

10. Bennour, J., Dugelay, J.-L.: Protection of 3D object through silhouette watermarking ICASSP 2006, 31st International Conference on Acoustics, Speech, and Signal Processing, Toulouse, France, May 14-19 (2006).
11. Cayre, F., Macq, B.: Data Hiding on 3D Triangle Meshes. IEEE Trans. on Signal Proc., **Vol. 51** (2003) 939–949.
12. Cayre, F., Rondao-Alface, P., Schmitt, F., Macq, B., Maître, H.: Application of Spectral Decomposition to Compression and Watermarking of 3D Triangle Mesh Geometry. Signal Processing: Image Communications, **18(4)** (2003) 309–319.
13. Cayre, F., Devillers, O., Schmitt, F., Maître, H.: Watermarking 3D Triangle Meshes for Authentication and Integrity, INRIA Research Report **RR-5223**, (2004).
14. Cignoni, P., Rocchini, C., Scopigno, R.: Metro: measuring error on simplified surfaces. Computer Graphics Forum, **17(2)** (1998) 167–174.
15. Corsini, M., Gelasca, E.D., Ebrahimi, T.: A multi-scale roughness metric for 3D watermarking quality assessment. Workshop on Image Analysis for Multimedia Interactive Services, April 13-15, Montreux, Switzerland (2005).
16. Cotting, D., Weyrich, T., Pauly, M., Gross, M.: Robust watermarking of point-sampled geometry. In Proc. of The International Conference on Shape Modeling and Applications (2004) 233-242.
17. Cox, I., Bloom, J., Miller, M.: Digital Watermarking, Principles & Practice. Morgan Kaufmann (2001).
18. Cho, J.W., Kim, M.S., Prost, R., Chung, H.Y., Jung, H.Y.: Robust watermarking on polygonal meshes using distribution of vertex norms. In Proc. of IWWM'05, LNCS 3304 of Lect Notes Comput Sc, Siena, Italy (2005) 283–293.
19. Denis, F., Lavoué, G., Dupont, F., Baskurt, A.: Digital Watermarking of Compressed 3D Meshes. Int. Conf. on Machine Intelligence, Tozeur, Tunisia, November 5-7 (2005).
20. Elad, A., Kimmel, R.: On Bending Invariant Signatures for Surfaces. IEEE Trans. on Pattern Analysis and Machine Intelligence **25(10)** (2003) 1285–1295.
21. Foley, J., van Dam, A., Feiner, S., Hughes, J.: Computer Graphics. Principle and Practice. Addison Wesley, Reading, MA. (1990).
22. Garcia, E., Dugelay, J.-L.: Texture-based watermarking of 3D video objects. IEEE Trans. Circuits Syst. Video Techn. **13(8)** (2003) 853–866.
23. Garland, M., Heckbert, P.S.: Surface simplification using quadric error metrics. In Proceedings of ACM SIGGRAPH (1997) 209-216.
24. Guskov, I., Sweldens, W., Schroder, P.: Multiresolution signal processing for meshes. In Proceedings ACM SIGGRAPH (1999) 325-334.
25. Harte, T., Bors A.: Watermarking 3D models. In Proc. of Int. Conf. on Image Proc. (ICIP), Rochester, NY, USA. (Sept. 2002).
26. Hoppe, H.: Progressive meshes. In Proc. of Computer Graphics SIGGRAPH (1996) 99–108.
27. Kanai, S., Date, D., Kishinami, T.: Digital watermarking for 3d p olygon using multiresolution wavelet decomposition. In Proc. Sixth IFIP WG 5.2 GEO-6, Tokyo, Japan (1998) 296-307.
28. Karni, Z., Gotsman, C.: Spectral compression of mesh geometry. In Proceedings ACM SIGGRAPH (2000) 279-286.
29. Kim, M.S., Valette, S., Jung, H.Y., Prost R.: Watermarking of 3D Irregular Meshes based on Wavelet Multiresolution Analysis. In Proceedings of IWWM'05, LNCS 3304 of Lect Notes Comput Sc, Siena, Italy (2005) 313–324.
30. Jin, J.Q., Dai, M.Y., Bao, H.J., Peng, Q.S.: Watermarking on 3D mesh based on spherical wavelet transform. SCI **5(3)** (2004) 251–258.

31. Lee, J.J., Cho, N.I., Kim, J.W.: Watermarking for 3D NURBS graphic data. IEEE Int. Workshop on MMSP02 (2002) 304–307.
32. Lounsbery, M., DeRose, T.D., Warren, J.: Multiresolution analysis for surfaces of arbitrary topological type. ACM Transactions on Graphics **16** (1997) 34-73.
33. Nikolaidis, A.,Tsekeridou, S., Tefas, A., Solachidis, V.: A Survey on Watermarking Application Scenarios and Related Attacks. In Proc. of International Conference of Image Processing **Vol. 3** (2001) 991–994.
34. Nielson, G., Foley, T.: Mathematical Methods in Computer Aided Geometric Design. Chapter A Survey of Applications of an Affine Invariant Norm, Academic Press, Boston. (1989) 445–467.
35. Ohbuchi, R., Masuda, H., Aono M.: Watermarking Three-Dimensional Polygonal Models Through Geometric and Topological Modifications. IEEE Jounal on Selected Areas in Communications **16(4)** (1998) 551–560.
36. Ohbuchi, R., Masuda, H., Aono, M.: A Shape-Preserving Data Embedding Algorithm for NURBS Curves and Surfaces. In Proc. of the Int. Conf. on Computer Graphics, June 07-11 (1999) 180–184.
37. Ohbuchi, R., Mukaiyama, A., Takahashi, S.: A Frequency-Domain Approach to Watermarking 3D Shapes. Computer Graphics Forum **21(3)** (2002) 373–382.
38. Page, D.L., Koschan, A.F., Sukumar, S.R., Roui-Abidi, B., Abidi, M.A.: Shape Analysis Algorithm Based on Information Theory. In Proc. of Int. Conf. on Image Processing, Barcelona, Spain **Vol. 1** (2003) 229–232.
39. Praun, E., Hoppe, H., Finkelstein, A.: Robust mesh watermarking. In Proceedings of the 26th annual conference on Computer graphics and interactive techniques. (1999) 49-56.
40. Prattichizzo, D., Barni, M., Tan, H.Z., Choi, S.: Perceptibility of Haptic Digital Watermarking of Virtual Textures. WHC (2005) 52–66.
41. Rondao Alface, P., Macq, B.: Blind Watermarking of 3D Meshes Using Robust Feature Points Detection. International Conference on Image Processing (ICIP05), Genova, Italy, 11-14 September **Vol. 1** (2005) 693–696.
42. Rondao Alface, P., Macq, B.: Shape Quality Measurement for 3D Watermarking Schemes. Electronic Imaging, Security and Watermarking of Multimedia Contents VIII, San Jose, California, 15-19 Jan. **Vol. 6072** (2006).
43. Schroder, P., Sweldens, W.: Spherical Wavelets: Efficiently Representing Functions on the Sphere. In Proc. of SIGGRAPH (1995) 161–172.
44. Surazhsky, V., Gotsman, C.: Explicit Surface Remeshing. In Proc. of the EUROGRAPHICS/ACM SIGGRAPH Symposium on Geometry Processing, ACM Press. (2003) 20–30.
45. Taubin, G.: A signal processing approach to fair surface design. Computer Graphics (SIGGRAPH 1995) **29** (1995) 351-358.
46. Uccheddu, F., Corsini, M., Barni, M.: Wavelet-based blind watermarking of 3D models. In Proc. of the 2004 Workshop on Multimedia and Security, Magdeburg, Germany (2004) 143–154.
47. Valette, S., Kim Y.S., Jung, H.Y., Magnin, I., Prost, R.: A multiresolution wavelet scheme for irregularly subdivided 3D triangular mesh. IEEE Int. Conf. on Image Processing, Kobe, Japan **1** (1999) 171–174.
48. Valette, S., Prost, R.: Multiresolution analysis of irregular surface meshes. IEEE Trans. Visual. Comput. Graphics **10** (2004) 113-122.
49. Voloshynovskiy, S., Pereira, S., Iquise, V., Pun T.: Attack modelling: towards a second generation watermarking benchmark. Signal Processing **81** (2001) 1177–1214.

50. Wagner, M.: Robust Watermarking of polygonal meshes. In Proc. of Geom. Mod. & Proc. (2000) 201–208.
51. Yeo, B.-L., Yeung, M.M.: Watermarking 3D Objects for Verification. IEEE Computer Graphics and Applications **19(1)** (1999) 36–45.
52. Yin, K., Pan, Z., Shi, J., Zhang, D.: Robust mesh watermarking based on multiresolution processing. Computers and Graphics **25** (2001) 409-420.
53. Yu, Z., Ip, H.H.S., Kwok, L.F.: A robust watermarking scheme for 3D triangular mesh models. Pattern Recognition **36(11)** (2003) 2603–2614.
54. Wang, C.M., Cheng, Y.M.: An Efficient Information Hiding Algorithm for Polygon Models. Computer Graphics Forum **24(3)** (2005) 591–600.
55. Wood, Z., Hoppe, H., Desbrun, M., Schröder,P.: Removing excess topology from isosurfaces. ACM Trans. on Graphics **23(2)** (2004) 190–208.
56. Wu, J., Kobbelt, L.: Efficient Spectral Watermarking of Large Meshes with Orthogonal Basis Functions. The Visual Computers (Pacific Graphics 2005 Proceedings), **21(8-10)** (2005) 848–857.
57. Zafeiriou, S., Tefas, A., Pitas, I.: Blind Robust Watermarking Schemes for Copyright Protection of 3D Mesh Objects. IEEE Trans. Vis. Comput. Graph. **11(5)** (2005) 596–607.
58. Zhang, H.: Discrete Combinatorial Laplacian Operators for Digital Geometry Processing. In Proc. of SIAM Conference on Geometric Design and Computing (2004) 575–592.
59. Zhou, L., Pang, A.: Metrics and Visualization Tools for Surface Mesh Comparison. In Proc. of SPIE conference on Visual Data Exploration and Analysis **Vol. 4302** (2001) 99-110.

Author Index

Adelsbach, André 1
Alface, Patrice Rondao 91

Chang, Ee-Chien 48

He, Shan 35
Huber, Ulrich 1

Kirovski, Darko 35

Liu, Fenlin 68

Luo, Xiangyang 68

Macq, Benoit 91

Sadeghi, Ahmad-Reza 1
Sun, Qibin 48

Wang, Daoshun 68

Yang, Chunfang 68
Ye, Shuiming 48

Lecture Notes in Computer Science

For information about Vols. 1–4447

please contact your bookseller or Springer

Vol. 4543: A.K. Bandara, M. Burgess (Eds.), Inter-Domain Management. XII, 237 pages. 2007.

Vol. 4542: P. Sawyer, B. Paech, P. Heymans (Eds.), Requirements Engineering: Foundation for Software Quality. IX, 384 pages. 2007.

Vol. 4541: T. Okadome, T. Yamazaki, M. Makhtari (Eds.), Pervasive Computing for Quality of Life Enhancemanet. IX, 248 pages. 2007.

Vol. 4539: N.H. Bshouty, C. Gentile (Eds.), Learning Theory. XII, 634 pages. 2007. (Sublibrary LNAI).

Vol. 4538: F. Escolano, M. Vento (Eds.), Graph-Based Representations in Pattern Recognition. XII, 416 pages. 2007.

Vol. 4537: K.C.-C. Chang, W. Wang, L. Chen, C.A. Ellis, C.-H. Hsu, A.C. Tsoi, H. Wang (Eds.), Advances in Web and Network Technologies, and Information Management. XXIII, 707 pages. 2007.

Vol. 4534: I. Tomkos, F. Neri, J. Solé Pareta, X. Masip Bruin, S. Sánchez Lopez (Eds.), Optical Network Design and Modeling. XI, 460 pages. 2007.

Vol. 4531: J. Indulska, K. Raymond (Eds.), Distributed Applications and Interoperable Systems. XI, 337 pages. 2007.

Vol. 4530: D.H. Akehurst, R. Vogel, R.F. Paige (Eds.), Model Driven Architecture- Foundations and Applications. X, 219 pages. 2007.

Vol. 4529: P. Melin, O. Castillo, L.T. Aguilar, J. Kacprzyk, W. Pedrycz (Eds.), Foundations of Fuzzy Logic and Soft Computing. XIX, 830 pages. 2007. (Sublibrary LNAI).

Vol. 4528: J. Mira, J.R. Álvarez (Eds.), Nature Inspired Problem-Solving Methods in Knowledge Engineering, Part II. XXII, 650 pages. 2007.

Vol. 4527: J. Mira, J.R. Álvarez (Eds.), Bio-inspired Modeling of Cognitive Tasks, Part I. XXII, 630 pages. 2007.

Vol. 4526: M. Malek, M. Reitenspieß, A. van Moorsel (Eds.), Service Availability. X, 155 pages. 2007.

Vol. 4525: C. Demetrescu (Ed.), Experimental Algorithms. XIII, 448 pages. 2007.

Vol. 4524: M. Marchiori, J.Z. Pan, C.d.S. Marie (Eds.), Web Reasoning and Rule Systems. XI, 382 pages. 2007.

Vol. 4523: Y.-H. Lee, H.-N. Kim, J. Kim, Y. Park, L.T. Yang, S.W. Kim (Eds.), Embedded Software and Systems. XIX, 829 pages. 2007.

Vol. 4522: B.K. Ersbøll, K.S. Pedersen (Eds.), Image Analysis. XVIII, 989 pages. 2007.

Vol. 4521: J. Katz, M. Yung (Eds.), Applied Cryptography and Network Security. XIII, 498 pages. 2007.

Vol. 4519: E. Franconi, M. Kifer, W. May (Eds.), The Semantic Web: Research and Applications. XVIII, 830 pages. 2007.

Vol. 4517: F. Boavida, E. Monteiro, S. Mascolo, Y. Koucheryavy (Eds.), Wired/Wireless Internet Communications. XIV, 382 pages. 2007.

Vol. 4516: L. Mason, T. Drwiega, J. Yan (Eds.), Managing Traffic Performance in Converged Networks. XXIII, 1191 pages. 2007.

Vol. 4515: M. Naor (Ed.), Advances in Cryptology - EUROCRYPT 2007. XIII, 591 pages. 2007.

Vol. 4514: S.N. Artemov, A. Nerode (Eds.), Logical Foundations of Computer Science. XI, 513 pages. 2007.

Vol. 4513: M. Fischetti, D.P. Williamson (Eds.), Integer Programming and Combinatorial Optimization. IX, 500 pages. 2007.

Vol. 4510: P. Van Hentenryck, L. Wolsey (Eds.), Integration of AI and OR Techniques in Constraint Programming for Combinatorial Optimization Problems. X, 391 pages. 2007.

Vol. 4509: Z. Kobti, D. Wu (Eds.), Advances in Artificial Intelligence. XII, 552 pages. 2007. (Sublibrary LNAI).

Vol. 4508: M.-Y. Kao, X.-Y. Li (Eds.), Algorithmic Aspects in Information and Management. VIII, 428 pages. 2007.

Vol. 4507: F. Sandoval, A. Prieto, J. Cabestany, M. Graña (Eds.), Computational and Ambient Intelligence. XXVI, 1167 pages. 2007.

Vol. 4506: D. Zeng, I. Gotham, K. Komatsu, C. Lynch, M. Thurmond, D. Madigan, B. Lober, J. Kvach, H. Chen (Eds.), Intelligence and Security Informatics: Biosurveillance. XI, 234 pages. 2007.

Vol. 4505: G. Dong, X. Lin, W. Wang, Y. Yang, J.X. Yu (Eds.), Advances in Data and Web Management. XXII, 896 pages. 2007.

Vol. 4504: J. Huang, R. Kowalczyk, Z. Maamar, D. Martin, I. Müller, S. Stoutenburg, K.P. Sycara (Eds.), Service-Oriented Computing: Agents, Semantics, and Engineering. X, 175 pages. 2007.

Vol. 4501: J. Marques-Silva, K.A. Sakallah (Eds.), Theory and Applications of Satisfiability Testing – SAT 2007. XI, 384 pages. 2007.

Vol. 4500: N. Streitz, A. Kameas, I. Mavrommati (Eds.), The Disappearing Computer. XVIII, 304 pages. 2007.

Vol. 4499: Y.Q. Shi (Ed.), Transactions on Data Hiding and Multimedia Security II. IX, 117 pages. 2007.

Vol. 4497: S.B. Cooper, B. Löwe, A. Sorbi (Eds.), Computation and Logic in the Real World. XVIII, 826 pages. 2007.

Vol. 4496: N.T. Nguyen, A. Grzech, R.J. Howlett, L.C. Jain (Eds.), Agent and Multi-Agent Systems: Technologies and Applications. XXI, 1046 pages. 2007. (Sublibrary LNAI).

Vol. 4495: J. Krogstie, A. Opdahl, G. Sindre (Eds.), Advanced Information Systems Engineering. XVI, 606 pages. 2007.

Vol. 4494: H. Jin, O.F. Rana, Y. Pan, V.K. Prasanna (Eds.), Algorithms and Architectures for Parallel Processing. XIV, 508 pages. 2007.

Vol. 4493: D. Liu, S. Fei, Z. Hou, H. Zhang, C. Sun (Eds.), Advances in Neural Networks – ISNN 2007, Part III. XXVI, 1215 pages. 2007.

Vol. 4492: D. Liu, S. Fei, Z. Hou, H. Zhang, C. Sun (Eds.), Advances in Neural Networks – ISNN 2007, Part II. XXVII, 1321 pages. 2007.

Vol. 4491: D. Liu, S. Fei, Z.-G. Hou, H. Zhang, C. Sun (Eds.), Advances in Neural Networks – ISNN 2007, Part I. LIV, 1365 pages. 2007.

Vol. 4490: Y. Shi, G.D. van Albada, J. Dongarra, P.M.A. Sloot (Eds.), Computational Science – ICCS 2007, Part IV. XXXVII, 1211 pages. 2007.

Vol. 4489: Y. Shi, G.D. van Albada, J. Dongarra, P.M.A. Sloot (Eds.), Computational Science – ICCS 2007, Part III. XXXVII, 1257 pages. 2007.

Vol. 4488: Y. Shi, G.D. van Albada, J. Dongarra, P.M.A. Sloot (Eds.), Computational Science – ICCS 2007, Part II. XXXV, 1251 pages. 2007.

Vol. 4487: Y. Shi, G.D. van Albada, J. Dongarra, P.M.A. Sloot (Eds.), Computational Science – ICCS 2007, Part I. LXXXI, 1275 pages. 2007.

Vol. 4486: M. Bernardo, J. Hillston (Eds.), Formal Methods for Performance Evaluation. VII, 469 pages. 2007.

Vol. 4485: F. Sgallari, A. Murli, N. Paragios (Eds.), Scale Space and Variational Methods in Computer Vision. XV, 931 pages. 2007.

Vol. 4484: J.-Y. Cai, S.B. Cooper, H. Zhu (Eds.), Theory and Applications of Models of Computation. XIII, 772 pages. 2007.

Vol. 4483: C. Baral, G. Brewka, J. Schlipf (Eds.), Logic Programming and Nonmonotonic Reasoning. IX, 327 pages. 2007. (Sublibrary LNAI).

Vol. 4482: A. An, J. Stefanowski, S. Ramanna, C.J. Butz, W. Pedrycz, G. Wang (Eds.), Rough Sets, Fuzzy Sets, Data Mining and Granular Computing. XIV, 585 pages. 2007. (Sublibrary LNAI).

Vol. 4481: J. Yao, P. Lingras, W.-Z. Wu, M. Szczuka, N.J. Cercone, D. Ślęzak (Eds.), Rough Sets and Knowledge Technology. XIV, 576 pages. 2007. (Sublibrary LNAI).

Vol. 4480: A. LaMarca, M. Langheinrich, K.N. Truong (Eds.), Pervasive Computing. XIII, 369 pages. 2007.

Vol. 4479: I.F. Akyildiz, R. Sivakumar, E. Ekici, J.C.d. Oliveira, J. McNair (Eds.), NETWORKING 2007. Ad Hoc and Sensor Networks, Wireless Networks, Next Generation Internet. XXVII, 1252 pages. 2007.

Vol. 4478: J. Martí, J.M. Benedí, A.M. Mendonça, J. Serrat (Eds.), Pattern Recognition and Image Analysis, Part II. XXVII, 657 pages. 2007.

Vol. 4477: J. Martí, J.M. Benedí, A.M. Mendonça, J. Serrat (Eds.), Pattern Recognition and Image Analysis, Part I. XXVII, 625 pages. 2007.

Vol. 4476: V. Gorodetsky, C. Zhang, V.A. Skormin, L. Cao (Eds.), Autonomous Intelligent Systems: Multi-Agents and Data Mining. XIII, 323 pages. 2007. (Sublibrary LNAI).

Vol. 4475: P. Crescenzi, G. Prencipe, G. Pucci (Eds.), Fun with Algorithms. X, 273 pages. 2007.

Vol. 4474: G. Prencipe, S. Zaks (Eds.), Structural Information and Communication Complexity. XI, 342 pages. 2007.

Vol. 4472: M. Haindl, J. Kittler, F. Roli (Eds.), Multiple Classifier Systems. XI, 524 pages. 2007.

Vol. 4471: P. Cesar, K. Chorianopoulos, J.F. Jensen (Eds.), Interactive TV: a Shared Experience. XIII, 236 pages. 2007.

Vol. 4470: Q. Wang, D. Pfahl, D.M. Raffo (Eds.), Software Process Dynamics and Agility. XI, 346 pages. 2007.

Vol. 4469: K.-C. Hui, Z. Pan, R.C.-k. Chung, C.C.L. Wang, X. Jin, S. Göbel, E.C.-L. Li (Eds.), Technologies for E-Learning and Digital Entertainment. XVIII, 974 pages. 2007.

Vol. 4468: M.M. Bonsangue, E.B. Johnsen (Eds.), Formal Methods for Open Object-Based Distributed Systems. X, 317 pages. 2007.

Vol. 4467: A.L. Murphy, J. Vitek (Eds.), Coordination Models and Languages. X, 325 pages. 2007.

Vol. 4466: F.B. Sachse, G. Seemann (Eds.), Functional Imaging and Modeling of the Heart. XV, 486 pages. 2007.

Vol. 4465: T. Chahed, B. Tuffin (Eds.), Network Control and Optimization. XIII, 305 pages. 2007.

Vol. 4464: E. Dawson, D.S. Wong (Eds.), Information Security Practice and Experience. XIII, 361 pages. 2007.

Vol. 4463: I. Măndoiu, A. Zelikovsky (Eds.), Bioinformatics Research and Applications. XV, 653 pages. 2007. (Sublibrary LNBI).

Vol. 4462: D. Sauveron, K. Markantonakis, A. Bilas, J.-J. Quisquater (Eds.), Information Security Theory and Practices. XII, 255 pages. 2007.

Vol. 4459: C. Cérin, K.-C. Li (Eds.), Advances in Grid and Pervasive Computing. XVI, 759 pages. 2007.

Vol. 4453: T. Speed, H. Huang (Eds.), Research in Computational Molecular Biology. XVI, 550 pages. 2007. (Sublibrary LNBI).

Vol. 4452: M. Fasli, O. Shehory (Eds.), Agent-Mediated Electronic Commerce. VIII, 249 pages. 2007. (Sublibrary LNAI).

Vol. 4451: T.S. Huang, A. Nijholt, M. Pantic, A. Pentland (Eds.), Artifical Intelligence for Human Computing. XVI, 359 pages. 2007. (Sublibrary LNAI).

Vol. 4450: T. Okamoto, X. Wang (Eds.), Public Key Cryptography – PKC 2007. XIII, 491 pages. 2007.

Vol. 4448: M. Giacobini et al. (Ed.), Applications of Evolutionary Computing. XXIII, 755 pages. 2007.